Maternal Fitness

PREPARING FOR THE MARATHON OF LABOR

Julie Tupler, R.N.
with Andrea Thompson

A FIRESIDE BOOK Published by Simon & Schuster
New York London Toronto Sydney Tokyo Singapore

F

FIRESIDE
Rockefeller Center
1230 Avenue of the Americas
New York, NY 10020

Designed by Bonni Leon-Berman
Illustrations by Kevin Pyle

Manufactured in the United States of America

7 9 10 8

Library of Congress Cataloging-in-Publication Data
Tupler, Julie.
    Maternal fitness : preparing for the marathon of labor / Julie
Tupler, with Andrea Thompson.
        p.   cm.
    "A Fireside book."
    Includes index.
    1. Pregnancy.   2. Exercise for women.   I. Thompson, Andrea.
    II. Title.
    RG558.7.T87   1996
    618.2'4—dc20   95-51221
CIP

ISBN 0-684-80295-3

This book is dedicated to the memory
of my mom and best friend
FLORENCE URIST TUPLER,
who with her wisdom, sense of humor,
and unconditional love prepared me for the
"marathon of life."

ACKNOWLEDGMENTS

I would like to thank Andrea, my editor Becky, Kevin, Jennine, my sister Sharon, Betsy, and Russell for all their help in making this book a reality.

I would also like to acknowledge my family and friends for all their love and support during the process: My sister Susan, my partner Bruce, my friends Susan, Linda, Cyd, Lisa, Elizabeth, Carolyn, Annie, Flori, Claudia, Kitty, Heather . . . and of course my twin Spanky Vernon Tupler.

CONTENTS

CHAPTER 1

An Introduction

Are You Ready to Run a Marathon?

You have just learned, to your inexpressible delight, that you're pregnant. You've been to the obstetrician, gotten a clean bill of health for you and your still-peanut-sized growing baby, lined up a series of once-a-month checkups for the next seven or eight months. You have armed yourself with the latest information and best advice about vitamin supplements, eating for two, and everything else you should know about what to put and what not to put in your body.

You've marked on your calendar the date, five months hence, when you and your partner will appear, pillows in hand, for the first of four childbirth education classes at the hospital or the nurse's office. You've canvassed friends who have been through childbirth to come up with a list of pregnancy exercise classes, and you're planning to sign up for the mothers-to-be workout group that meets once a week at the Y. You're ready. You've got your bases covered. So why do you need this book?

First, all that other stuff is great. Of course you should keep regular appointments with your doctor and learn as much as you can about the birth process and join an exercise group. But consider this: you should spend perhaps twenty minutes a month with your obstetrician, at least until the very end of your pregnancy, and he or she will be interested mainly in monitoring vital signs and making sure all systems are go.

Childbirth education sessions will teach you some techniques, mostly about breathing, that you may or may not find useful when the time comes (just ask a friend who's had a baby). Group exercise classes are designed to provide general workouts for a roomful of women. Not one of these supports, essential or helpful though it may be, will show you *how to prepare your body* for your pregnancy and your labor. That's what we'll do. In particular and most important, the Maternal Fitness routine will show you how to strengthen the most important pregnancy muscles of all, the abdominals.

Decades ago my neighbor gave birth to her oldest child, and recently I asked this healthy, strong, charming, articulate, feisty seventy-five-year-old, "How did it go? What was it like?" Here's some of what she told me: "Everybody—my doctor, my mother, my aunt—said, 'Don't move around too much. Don't raise your arms over your head to get things down from a top shelf; you'll shift the baby and maybe start contractions. Don't lift anything heavy; you'll strain your muscles and maybe start contractions. Don't stand on your feet too long. Don't run unless the house is burning down.'

"Labor pains started, and my husband took me to the hospital," she continued. "A gas cone was put over my mouth and nose, and I woke up—who knows when?—the mother of a son. Then I stayed in the hospital for two weeks. I felt perfectly fine, but that's what new mothers did in those days. Flat on my back for one week. Then I was allowed to sit on the edge of the bed and dangle my legs over the side. Then, finally, walking!"

Not an unusual story. That's what having a baby was like for many women in our grandmothers' and even our mothers' time: Something that other people, the experts, took charge of. Something of a medical "problem," like coming down with a bad case of the flu or dropping a bowling ball on your foot. Something that brought down on the poor pregnant woman's head a flurry of old wives' tales about what she had to do or must never do with her body if she wanted to end up with a baby.

Some of that stuff *might* apply if you're an old wife, a *really* old wife—say, seventy or eighty—and pregnant. Fortunately, over the last several decades there's been a sea change, nothing short of a revolution, really, in attitudes about pregnancy and childbirth. It's a revolution that we—the women having the kids—have played a big part in, because we started saying, "Hey! I'm strong, I'm healthy, I want to have a baby, I *am* having a baby, and I don't need a lot of people telling me how to do it." We said, "I'm proud of my big, beautiful, bulging body. I want to be awake and alert and fully engaged in giving birth. I want my partner with me in the delivery room and my baby in my arms right away, not whisked off to a nursery down the hall. I want to get up and out and back to my life, my family, my job, my clothes, my workouts.

The medical profession has changed along with us. Obstetricians and family practice doctors are saying it's good for a pregnant woman to keep fit and strong, keep with an exercise regimen if that's what she's been accustomed to. Indeed, more and more, exercise is being promoted as an essential part of good prenatal care—just as important for feeling good and producing a healthy baby as eating the right foods, avoiding the bad stuff, getting enough sleep, and going for checkups. A report by Dr. James F. Clapp even suggests that exercising during pregnancy makes for a better delivery. According to one study, almost nine out of ten who exercised had their babies without obstetric interventions—no forceps, no cesareans—while among the non-exercisers, that figure was only about 50 percent. To my way of thinking, it's common sense: the better shape you're in, the better you'll handle those nine months while you're growing a new life inside you and on that spectacular day when you welcome your new son or daughter to join you in the world outside. One thing is for sure: having a baby is the most phenomenal thing your body will ever do.

Over the past five years I have led hundreds of pregnant women through an exercise routine that I have developed and refined with three goals in mind.

The first goal is *prevention*. You don't need me or anybody else to point out this basic fact: from the day of conception through the next nine months your body undergoes dramatic changes and unusual stresses. Your breasts get bigger, pulling your shoulders and head forward, shortening your chest muscles, and lengthening your upper back muscles. Your belly gets bigger, compelling you to compensate for this startling change in your center of gravity by curving in your spine in ways it never did before. Your hormones run riot, causing your joints to loosen, and you to feel oddly unstable on your feet. Your growing uterus presses on lungs and bladder and anything else in its way, creating surprising difficulties when you try to do normal things, like breathe. The result: backaches, shoulder aches, neck aches, urinary incontinence, and all the other non-serious but unattractive and sometimes painful problems that so many pregnant women know so well.

In this book you'll learn how to prevent most of these discomforts. My exercises will show you how to align and balance the different parts of your changing body, how to lengthen muscles that keep getting shorter, and how to shorten muscles getting longer.

The second goal is *preparation*. I tell a particularly fitness-minded client to think of preparing for childbirth as she would for running a twenty-mile race. Think of it as the marathon of labor. Not to scare her but to help her get in a mind-set that says delivering a baby is—among many other glorious things, of course—an athletic event, one she can and should prepare for by understanding what is involved, what a truly *bodily* business it is. The analogy to the long-distance run is apt. Preparing for child-birth is a grind! Labor and birth take the same kind of focus, strength, and stamina, which means that before the main event, you need to do some training. That's something you don't hear a lot about in prenatal classes.

Here's what you *do* typically learn in the traditional childbirth class: during contractions you should breathe in various ways and combinations of ways; during delivery you should hold your breath and bear down.

I say, before your baby is ready to be born, breathe in any way that works to help you through contractions. And when it's time to deliver, keep right on breathing, and work your strong abdominal muscles to push that baby out like toothpaste out of a tube! That's what the most critical exercises in this book will show you—how to strengthen your transverse muscle gradually over nine months (the transverse is your innermost abdominal muscle; it circles your waist like a wide belt and goes forward and backward when you breathe) and how to use it to push *back* on the uterus when the time comes to push. I call this "the Tupler Technique," because it's unique to my pregnancy workout program.

The abdominals aren't the only muscles that need preparation. For one thing, childbirth, for the majority of women in this country, happens while a woman is lying supine. That's a strain on the legs, especially the long muscles of the inner and outer thighs. I'll show you how to strengthen those muscles so you'll avoid the kind of leg fatigue that's a distraction you don't need when you're concentrating on getting that baby out.

You'll learn here, too, how to control the muscles of the pelvic floor so that you will be able to relax and open them while your abdominals are doing that tightening and pushing back against the uterus.

Relaxation is an overlooked, misunderstood, and most critical component of fitness, by the way. Maybe it's not talked about much because it sounds like something that should come naturally. Nurses or doctors will tell you, when you're in a lot of pain, "Just relax!" The fact is that it's hard to *just relax,* and you need to *learn* how to do it!

And the third goal is *restoration.* Childbirth is the end of pregnancy, of course, and the beginning of everything else. During the postpartum weeks, your body will be adjusting once again—to another change in the center of gravity, stretched muscles, and more—and all that is going on while you're feeding, carrying, and generally doing everything else for your new baby. The difficulties of this period of adjustment should not be underestimated! The more you work the critical muscles *while* you're pregnant, the lesser your chances of developing backaches, shoulder pain, and other aches *after* you're pregnant.

Again I think it's just common sense that the more thoughtfully you exercise your body during pregnancy, the faster and more easily it will recover, or restore itself to your pre-pregnancy shape and energy level.

Three Women, Three Stories

Carmen, thirty-eight years old when she became pregnant with her first child, was in the pink of health and very fit. Carmen doesn't exercise because she thinks she should or because she knows it makes her look better. She does it because she loves every sweating, huffing, grinding minute of it! A naturally talented athlete with a long, agile body, she's always been a serious skier and a serious tennis player, and she's a recent convert to in-line skating. She hits the gym two or three times a week for step classes and workouts with the weight machines. "I'm an addict, what can I tell you?" says Carmen about her fitness fanaticism.

Claudia, pregnant with twins, her second and third children, at age twenty-five, said that "running around like a crazy woman"—mainly on the trail of her three-year-old-son—was her major form of physical workout. (In fact, she does have powerful leg muscles.) The only time Claudia "officially" exercised was in an aerobics class at the Y when she first got out of college. She describes herself as "a little on the pudgy side" and "the original klutz of the Western world."

Frances, age thirty, had her first baby by cesarean section and was eager to deliver his new brother or sister vaginally. Because she was never much of an exerciser to begin with, her upper and lower body strength was weak and she tired fairly easily. Although her pregnancy was normal and proceeded smoothly, the sciatic nerve in her right leg was irritated by the way she carried her baby, and Frances experienced a fair degree of pain when walking or lying down.

Carmen, Claudia, and Frances were all clients of mine. All followed the exercise routine you'll find in this book, and they say they felt better and stronger each day. All had uncomplicated births and robust babies. Frances surprised her obstetrician and delighted herself by a vaginal delivery that she reports was "almost a piece of cake!" Carmen pushed her daughter out in eight minutes, was up and walking around one hour later, and went back to wearing her prenatal skirts three weeks after that. Claudia says she feels "amazingly lean and mean, after a much more comfortable pregnancy than I had the first time around."

My point is this: exercising during pregnancy is *good* for you, you *can* do it, and you *will* learn some new and most useful techniques from this book. My program works for everyone, and it will work for you if you're over thirty-five and having your first child, if you've been letting your muscles just lie there for years, if you're a fitness fiend already, if you've had an earlier cesarean, or if your body is playing tricks on you and throwing in some discomforts you weren't told to expect. Of course, there are some movements you should avoid, some signals that tell you to slow down or stop. You'll learn here what those are, and you'll feel confident in your own ability to listen to your body.

Adjust the routine to your own fitness level and preferences—it's simple and I'll show you how. I want this book to feel and function as if you have invited me or one of my trainers into your home for a personal, one-on-one workout designed to meet your one-of-a-kind needs. Will it be fun? I hope so—or at least a feeling-good way to work your body during these amazing months.

CHAPTER 2

The Tupler Technique

Getting to Know the Muscles You'll Need

Suppose you're planning a long-distance bike ride. It's going to be a hard-driving trip toward a specific destination. What would you do to prepare? You'd strengthen those leg muscles that will be worked to the max and practice that pedaling movement that will get you where you're going.

That's what I want you to do to get ready for the marathon of labor—strengthen your muscles and practice the movements you'll be using. In fact, I want you to strengthen, strengthen, strengthen and practice, practice, practice!

In Chapters 7 and 8 you'll learn the exercises that will enable you to prepare for labor. You'll be shown how to strengthen the muscles that are most vigorously involved in childbirth: the abdominals (in particular, the transverse) and the pubococcygeus, or PC, the main muscle of the pelvic floor. You'll learn how to practice using these muscles in the way you should be using them when you're ready to deliver—getting that baby out by squeezing back on top and relaxing and opening down below.

That's what the Tupler Technique is all about. We're not just talking exercises here to make you feel or look better, although they certainly will do that. The Tupler Technique involves three elements that together—if you learn them and practice them as religiously as you brush your teeth every day—constitute a *skill* you will need when you're ready to give birth.

Here are the elements of the Tupler Technique:

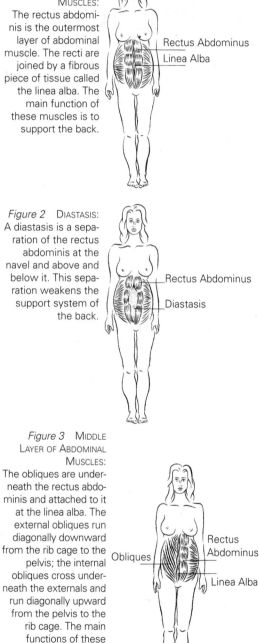

Figure 1 OUTER-MOST ABDOMINAL MUSCLES: The rectus abdominis is the outermost layer of abdominal muscle. The recti are joined by a fibrous piece of tissue called the linea alba. The main function of these muscles is to support the back.

Rectus Abdominus
Linea Alba

Figure 2 DIASTASIS: A diastasis is a separation of the rectus abdominis at the navel and above and below it. This separation weakens the support system of the back.

Rectus Abdominus
Diastasis

Figure 3 MIDDLE LAYER OF ABDOMINAL MUSCLES: The obliques are underneath the rectus abdominis and attached to it at the linea alba. The external obliques run diagonally downward from the rib cage to the pelvis; the internal obliques cross underneath the externals and run diagonally upward from the pelvis to the rib cage. The main functions of these muscles are flexing of the trunk and turning from side to side.

Obliques
Rectus Abdominus
Linea Alba

- breathing the right way
- working a strengthened transverse muscle
- relaxing a strengthened PC muscle

That's what I teach clients in my Maternal Fitness program, and that's what will get you through a great delivery and a speedy post-birth shape up.

Anatomy 101

Here's a short lesson in musculature, so we know what we're talking about.

Your abdominal muscles lie (surprise!) in your abdomen. You have three sets of abdominals—the rectus abdominis, the obliques, and the transverse.

The *rectus abdominis* (see Figure 1) is the outermost muscle. It runs up and down and has two halves, called the *recti,* that are normally about half an inch apart and are joined together by a fibrous piece of tissue called the *linea alba.* During pregnancy, the increasing bulk of the uterus pushing out against the recti can cause the two halves to become longer and to separate around the belly button area (see Figure 2). This is called a *diastasis,* and most women tend to develop one during pregnancy. (In Chapter 6 I'll show you how to check yourself for a diastasis.) This diastasis does not threaten the baby in any way, but it is a major cause of that aching back you might experience during and after pregnancy. (More in the following chapter about diastasis.)

The *obliques* are underneath the rectus abdominis and are attached to it at the linea alba at the bottom (see Figure 3). The external obliques run diagonally downward from the rib cage to the pelvis; the internal obliques cross underneath the externals and run diagonally upward from the pelvis to the rib cage. The obliques are the muscles that enable you to flex your trunk and to turn laterally—that is, from side to side.

Finally, the *transverse,* as its name suggests, goes straight across the abdomen, like a corset. It is attached to your bottom six ribs, to the top of your pelvis in back (see Figure 4), and to the recti in front at the linea alba (see Figure 5). Put your hands on your belly above and below your belly button and take a big breath so that your belly expands. The muscle you feel going out and then in, forward and then backward, is your transverse. It is my favorite muscle. It should be your favorite muscle. Why? Because this is the muscle you're going to use to push your baby out.

The abdominals are the muscles up on top. The ones down below are in the pelvic floor. If you think of your pelvis as a bag of groceries, the pelvic floor is the bottom of the bag. The main muscle of the pelvic floor, the *PC,* short for *pubococcygeus,* lies in a figure eight around the openings to the urethra, the vagina, and the rectum (see Figures 6 and 7).

Get in touch with that pelvic floor muscle now by pretending to stop your flow of urine, or go into the bathroom to urinate and actually interrupt the urine flow. That muscle you're pulling in is your PC. However—and I'll say this again later—when we get going on the exercises, you should *not* do PC-strengthening exercises, or *kegels, while* you're urinating, because that will increase your chances of developing a urinary tract infection. It's okay to do the urine-stopping squeeze now just to identify the muscle to yourself.

The first function of the pelvic floor muscle is support for what's inside the pelvis—support for the

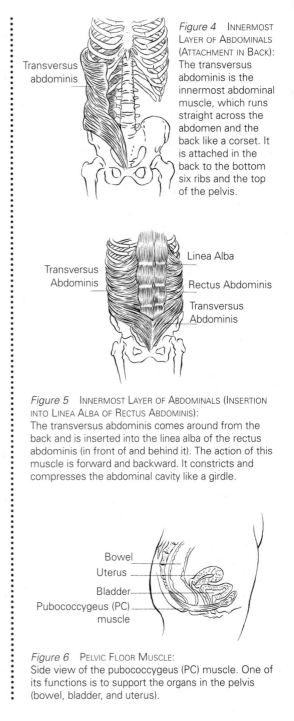

Figure 4 INNERMOST LAYER OF ABDOMINALS (ATTACHMENT IN BACK): The transversus abdominis is the innermost abdominal muscle, which runs straight across the abdomen and the back like a corset. It is attached in the back to the bottom six ribs and the top of the pelvis.

Figure 5 INNERMOST LAYER OF ABDOMINALS (INSERTION INTO LINEA ALBA OF RECTUS ABDOMINIS): The transversus abdominis comes around from the back and is inserted into the linea alba of the rectus abdominis (in front of and behind it). The action of this muscle is forward and backward. It constricts and compresses the abdominal cavity like a girdle.

Figure 6 PELVIC FLOOR MUSCLE: Side view of the pubococcygeus (PC) muscle. One of its functions is to support the organs in the pelvis (bowel, bladder, and uterus).

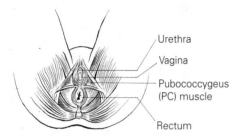

Figure 7 Pelvic Floor
Muscle:
Back-lying view of the
PC muscle. It forms a
figure eight around the
urethra, vagina, and
rectum.

Urethra

Vagina

Pubococcygeus
(PC) muscle

Rectum

Figure 8 Pushing:
Pushing during labor is
like squeezing tooth-
paste out of a tube.
The transversus abdo-
minis (your hand)
pushes back against
the uterus (the tube),
and the baby, like
toothpaste, comes
happily out the bottom!

"groceries." Another function is to enable elimination, and a third is to aid sexual enjoyment. We'll
talk about all that some more in the following chapter, but here I want to explain a fourth function.
What does the PC have to do with preparing for the
marathon of labor? Why is the PC part and parcel of
the Tupler Technique?

When you're in labor, ideally you will work the
transverse and the PC muscles *separately*—squeezing in with the transverse to push back on the
uterus, opening and relaxing the PC to let the baby
out. Here's another image I offer my clients: Pushing while giving birth is like getting toothpaste out
of a tube (see Figure 8). The transverse pushing
back on the uterus is like your hand squeezing the
tube; the baby, like toothpaste, comes out the bottom. If you tighten the transverse and the PC at the
same time, you're keeping the cap on the tube—not
the best way to let the contents out!

As you do the exercises, you will be isolating and
separating these muscles—relaxing your abdominals as you work the pelvic floor muscles, and vice
versa. (The only time to hold the transverse and the
PC in simultaneously is when you sneeze or cough,
so you don't pee on your shoes.)

Does something seem strange here? Why, you're
asking, should you strengthen the PC muscle if the
point is to relax it? Aren't you going to get too tight
down there if you pump this muscle? No. What are
you going to do, develop bulk? I don't think so.

If you strengthen your arm muscle, you can still
relax it, can't you? It's the same thing with your
pelvic floor muscles. Although it may sound para-
doxical, a strengthened muscle stretches more easily and more completely. In the pelvic floor
exercises you will strengthen the muscle and then
practice relaxing it. You will practice *seeing* it open

up like a flower—another image I'm fond of. Whenever you urinate or have a bowel movement, you naturally, unconsciously, relax the PC; I want you to become *conscious* of that muscle, so that you will recognize what it feels like when it's open. Developing that mind-body awareness will enable you to relax and open the pelvic floor during labor.

So now you know your muscles. Now learn to love them!

Power from the Center

Conventional thinking says you should be gentle with your pregnant abdominals, go easy on that bulging midsection, don't put pressure on the baby. This is, in my opinion, about as out-of-date and misguided as telling a healthy pregnant woman she shouldn't work and should never lift anything over her head.

You cannot harm your baby by exercising your transverse muscle. Your baby is very well protected inside your uterus. As you work your transverse from front to back in the way I'll show you, your baby might be getting a little aerobics session, but he or she is not in any danger.

I hope I've convinced you by now that strengthening the transverse is critical for labor. Giving birth is a power workout if ever there was one, and the more you get that power coming from the center, the better off you'll be. As you do the exercises I'll teach you in Chapter 7 and Chapter 8, you'll be working the transverse through all the movements and positions (except when you're relaxing the abdominals to work the PC muscle). Your transverse will be *in* "on the work"—that is, when you are executing a particular movement—and when you're doing a leg lift or an arm lift, I will ask you to think of the transverse lifting that leg or lifting that arm. Think: power from the center!

Abdominals: The Missing Link

During pregnancy, if you develop a diastasis and the backaches that usually go along with it, you'll discover the benefits of strengthening the transverse muscle. And a strong transverse is going to be your greatest ally during labor.

Right now I want you to learn to love your transverse for another reason: if you work my favorite muscle the right way, you'll slip back into your pre-pregnancy skirts and jeans very early on in your postpartum days. Transverse work helps to give you flat abdominals. I tell clients: "If I don't lure you in on the need to get ready to push during birth or on the wonders you can do for your back, I'm going to get you on your vanity! Because the more diligently you strengthen the muscle during pregnancy, the faster you'll get your shape back afterward."

In fact, transverse exercises are the missing link in abdominal work for everybody, whether you're trying to shape up during or after pregnancy or have never had a baby in your life. Many serious exercises will do sit-ups for years and not understand why they still have those little midsection pouches and flabbies. This happens because they're doing abdominals wrong—not bringing the transverse *in*.

In a gym, typically, you're instructed to do sit-ups by inhaling, then exhaling as you execute the move—but if you exhale and rise up without first bringing the transverse in, you're making *that muscle* pop out, and that means it's getting longer and weaker. If you strengthen the transverse first through the routine you'll learn in Chapter 7, sit-ups will become a piece of cake. Because I sometimes do a couple of thousand transverse squeezes a day, I can easily manage a couple of hundred sit-ups at a time without strain.

Breathing for Strength

Breathing correctly, as I said, is the third element in the Tupler Technique. Although I'm talking about it here at the end, it is actually the beginning of exercising properly and a critical component of all the movements you will do during your workouts. But what is there to learn? Breathing is . . . well, as easy as breathing, right?

Not necessarily. If I tell you to inhale, what do you do? If you're like most people, chances are you suck in your tummy and lift your shoulders as you suck in air. This is called breathing in opposition, and it's the wrong way to inhale. For one thing, you're involving only a small part of your lungs and thus getting less oxygen; for another, you're using your abdominal muscles incorrectly.

As I said when we were talking about doing sit-ups, if you have spent any time working out in a gym you've no doubt been advised to exhale "on the work," or as you are executing a particular movement, in order to avoid holding your breath. This is good advice. But if you suck *in* your abdominal muscles as you inhale, you will push them *out* as you exhale—as you "do the work." For anybody, that's a wrong way to breathe and a wrong way to exercise; for a pregnant woman, it's disastrous, because you will be pushing forward against the recti, the two halves of your outer-most abdominal muscle. The recti are already being lengthened and pushed apart by your growing uterus. More pushing against them by improper breathing during exercise will further weaken the recti and increase your chances of developing backaches.

I want you to get into the habit of *diaphragmatic breathing,* or expanding your belly as you inhale. When you start the exercises described in Chapter 7, you'll see this called a "belly breath," and it is the beginning of every muscle-stretching or -strengthening move you'll be doing in the workout. A belly breath will get the greatest amount of oxygen to you and your baby as you exercise; it will give you staying power and help you relax. And belly breaths will help you keep your muscles working the way you want them to during delivery.

The American College of Obstetricians and Gynecologists (ACOG) is the nation's leading group of professionals providing health care for women. About 90 percent of American gynecologists and obstetricians are members, and one of the organizations's goals is to keep its members up to date on the latest developments in the field. In a bulletin entitled "Women and Exercise," ACOG makes this wonderfully clear and simple statement: "The more a muscle repeats an activity, the more efficient the muscle becomes. The more a group of muscles or several groups of muscles perform an activity, the more efficient that activity becomes."

Make your birthing muscles as efficient as they can get, and when all the activity starts, they'll serve you well.

That's why the Tupler Technique can help you prepare for the marathon of labor and delivery. Now you'll see how it can help you throughout the nine months leading up to the big moment.

CHAPTER 3

Going the Whole Nine Months

or What Happened to the Body I Used to Know and Love?

That call you've been waiting for comes from the doctor's office—"Congratulations, you're pregnant!"—and at once your body feels . . . different. Maybe it's been feeling different for a week or two already—a little puffier here, a little more tender there. You sense a sea change in the making. You sense correctly. Indeed, over the nine months to come, you may feel, increasingly, as if you're inhabiting a strange new-old state, a place you used to know well but where someone is now switching all the road signs on you.

Pregnancy is hard work leading to the even harder work of labor, a physical condition that places increased or brand-new stresses on your body. And not only up in front, where it eventually feels and looks as if you've strapped on and are carrying around an unusually heavy basketball.

Here's a closer look at what's going on (you'll recognize yourself in some if not all of these descriptions).

Your belly is bulging—or it soon will be. It takes approximately 280 days to make a baby. That's not long in terms of a lifetime, but it's an *eternity* when you're waiting ever more urgently for that baby to join you on the outside—and when he or she keeps getting bigger and bigger inside you.

By the sixth or seventh week, your baby—already starting to look like a little human being—is just about an inch long. Over the next three or four months, your

25

baby will grow at a galloping rate, and by the middle of the fifth month, he or she will be about ten inches long and will weigh about twelve ounces.

It's during the last trimester that your baby-in-the-making *really* starts taking over what once was your old familiar body. From the end of the seventh month—by which time all vital organs are formed—the baby's main job is to get longer and heavier. Midway through the eighth month, he or she will weigh about 3½ pounds; a month later your baby will have put on a couple more pounds and grown to 17 or 18 inches in length. Add in the weight of the placenta and amniotic fluid, and by the time you get close to delivery you'll be carrying around about 13½ pounds of baby.

Little Jason or Jennifer doesn't have much room! While your uterus is still up in the middle of your body, before it moves down into your pelvis shortly before birth, your baby is going to be pushing things around—your lungs and your stomach and anything else that's in the way. This doesn't exactly make you feel like running a road race.

Your breasts have taken on a life of their own. You may be thoroughly enjoying your newly lush and voluptuous curves, and why shouldn't you? Or perhaps you're watching those startling and ever-growing protuberances with alarm. Whichever, swelling breasts almost inevitably mean discomfort in various parts of your body. As your breasts get bigger, their weight tends to bring your shoulders forward, and then your rounded, forward-slumping shoulders bring your head along with them. This doesn't look too terrific, posture-wise. In addition, the muscles of the upper back are lengthening; you'll remember from Anatomy 101 that a muscle that's getting longer than it's supposed to be is getting weaker. So your growing breasts may be a part of the reason your back is so achy.

You can't stand up straight anymore. Or you've forgotten what standing up straight feels like. The swelling breasts, followed by the rounded shoulders and the drooping head, plus the bulging belly, are part of it. But only part. Here's what else is likely to be going on: Your neck and chin are poking forward. Your rib cage is squished in by slouching shoulders and chest. The top of your pelvis is tilting forward while your buttocks are popping out, and your back has assumed an *S*-shape, with a large inward curve in the lumbar, or lower, portion of the spine. Your feet are trying to maintain all this shifting by splaying out when you walk.

Your body adapts to the big belly, the growing breasts, and the other jutting-outs and swaying-ins that alter its center of gravity, and to certain hormonal changes (described later) that affect the stability of the joints, by realigning and rebalancing its various segments.

What it all means is that pregnancy may give you a posture that looks like this (see Figure 9). It gets harder to walk around. It gets harder to sit up and harder to stand up.

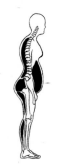

Your shoes don't fit anymore. Your feet are tired from carrying around your out-of-kilter body. The arches are strained. Your feet are puffy because blood and water are accumulating in them. They're most content when you put on an ancient, broken-in pair of slippers and pad gently around the house.

Figure 9   POOR POS-
TURE DURING PREGNANCY:
Head thrown forward,
shoulders rounded, and
lower back arched.

Your back aches. It hurts across your shoulders because of the forward pull of your breasts and head. In addition, if you have a diastasis—which, at least to some degree, you probably do—your middle and lower back feels stressed and strained, especially when you stand up and sit down, when you stand for a while, and when you walk. Remember how the recti, the two halves of the rectus abdominis muscle, tend to separate (that's a diastasis) because the uterus is pushing them apart? Because the recti are the major support system for your back, when they're apart and stretching out, they can't do that job well.

You're having trouble not urinating in your pants. Remember that the pubo-coccygeus, or PC, the main muscle of the pelvic floor, surrounds the urethra and rectum as well as the vagina. So one of its functions is to aid elimination: the PC innervates the sphincter muscles, allowing you to stop and start the flow of urine and to have a bowel movement.

As the nine months proceed and your uterus gets heavier, its pressure on the PC weakens the muscle. One result? Leaky urine when you sneeze or cough.

While all these structural-skeletal-muscular changes are going on, your hormones—especially estrogen, progesterone, and relaxin—are running riot and may be causing other changes:

You feel a little queasy, or a lot queasy. Changing levels of progesterone and estrogen in your body, especially during the first months of pregnancy, make you feel nauseated. The sight and smell—maybe even the thought—of once-favorite meals turn you green around the gills.

Hormonal changes also increase the probability that you'll have bouts of consti-pation, and *that* can make you more vulnerable to hemorrhoids, those stretched veins that occur around the anus and that make defecating or even just sitting extremely painful.

You feel pooped. Again, hormones, hormones, hormones. And the fatigue associated with carrying around added weight. In addition, you have more blood in your system. During pregnancy, the level of plasma (the liquid portion of blood) increases more than does the level of red cells. This is called physiologic anemia of pregnancy, and it's one of the reasons many women experience tiredness during the early months.

You may feel kind of loosey-goosey. Relaxin, one of the hormones produced by the body, is causing your ligaments to soften and stretch. When ligaments, the inelastic bands of connective tissue that help hold your joints together, soften and stretch, your joints relax and separate. This is not all bad. Your body knows what it's doing, because your pelvis must relax to accommodate your growing baby.

But that relaxin may also be affecting joints in your shoulders, elbows, wrists, hips, knees, and ankles. That can add to your backache woes, for one thing; for another, it can make you feel a little unstable on your feet, wobbly in the arms, and dismayingly clumsy as you go about your normal activities.

Connective tissue laxity and joint instability, added to the change in the body's center of gravity, make pregnant women more accident prone. And if you were physically active and very flexible before your pregnancy, relaxin will now make you even more flexible and thus at even greater risk of falling. That's a reason to approach with caution any sport or exercise that involves bouncy movements or quick changes in direction, such as step classes, tennis, skiing, and running.

You feel hot. In fact, you may feel perfectly comfortable in a cotton shirt and shorts in the middle of winter. This doesn't have to do with hormones, exactly. You feel hot because your inner core body temperature increases during pregnancy. And that requires some exercising precautions, which we'll talk about later, because when you exercise, your temperature goes up even higher. Your body can cool itself down by perspiring, but your baby's body can't. That's also why pregnant women should steer clear of saunas, hot tubs, and hot baths.

Put it all together and it's not a pretty picture, and very likely the last thing you feel like doing—or even thinking about—is exercising. But if you follow the Maternal Fitness program, you'll be doing yourself a big favor.

How the Maternal Fitness Program Will Make for a More Enjoyable Pregnancy

We all know by now—because only somebody who's been living under a rock for the past couple of decades could have missed the news—that exercise is a great form of preventive medicine, one that keeps our bodies healthy and increases our ability to weather the ordinary and extraordinary stresses of life. Pregnancy surely qualifies as a premier example of the latter. I promise you that the exercises you'll learn in Chapter 7 and Chapter 8—and that you'll do religiously—really will help you sail through these months feeling less stressed, more fit, more comfortable, and a lot stronger.

The routine will benefit your pregnant body in two ways: by stretching your muscles and by strengthening them.

You need to stretch those muscles that have been getting too short or tensed up. Stretching, in general and for anybody, is one of the simplest, quickest, cheapest ways to feel good. This is not just my opinion. Studies have shown that it's a great way to relieve muscle tension and stiffness, to reduce anxiety and stress, even to lower blood pressure and breathing rate. And if you exercise regularly or engage in sports, you already know that stretching beforehand helps you limber up and helps prevent muscle strain, and that stretching after your activity prevents muscles from tightening up.

So stretching is good for a lot of reasons. One of the special reasons it's good for you right now is that it enables you to lengthen those muscles that have been getting shorter and tighter in response to your changing shape, weight, and posture.

What do we want to stretch in the pregnant body? The exercises you'll be doing include movements to provide a gentle stretch for the pectorals, those upper chest muscles that have been squishing in, and pelvic tilts to lengthen the muscles of the lower back. These are going to help you straighten up your shoulders and head and make your back feel better.

In addition, you're going to do some moves to stretch out and relax those leg muscles—the adductor, or inner thigh, muscles, the hip flexors, and the hamstrings that run down the backs of your legs—which have been tightening up from the added weight they're carrying and from the probably weird way you're walking these days.

Stretching is also the way to maintain or improve flexibility, or the ability to move your joints through their range of motion. You'll do stretches to increase flexibility in your arms, legs, and back, and to help you bend, walk, and generally feel more comfortable when your body is in motion. But because of that hormonally induced joint laxity that hits many women in pregnancy, we'll do these exercises nice and easy, in a slow and controlled manner.

Your other goal is to shorten and strengthen those muscles that have been getting too stretched out or that are fatigued from the demands a pregnant body is placing on them.

Starting from the top, that means working on those muscles across your upper back, which are getting pulled forward and creating slouching shoulders and pain and fatigue in your upper back. If in addition to sustaining the inevitable body changes of pregnancy you're sitting hunched over at a desk all day, you almost certainly have a stretch weakness in your back.

Then of course—here comes my favorite again—you will be shortening and strengthening your abdominal muscles, especially the transverse. You know from the last chapter that the transverse is critical for labor. Besides that, it's going to help prevent back problems during these nine months.

Each time you exercise your transverse by bringing it in and back, you are also bringing the recti, the two vertical halves of muscle, back and together. You'll be shortening and strengthening these muscles from the middle, because during pregnancy the recti have been getting longer and longer. If you have a diastasis, or separation of the recti, you probably have back problems, as we said, because the rectus abdominis is part of the support system for your back and if it pulls apart it's not going to be very effective.

So . . . do your transverse exercises. They can prevent a diastasis if you start early in your pregnancy. If you already have one, they will help stop it from getting bigger and may even close it up.

You'll be doing squats and other exercises to work the muscles in your knees, calves, thighs, and buttocks. By strengthening those long outer thigh muscles you'll help do away with the pregnant waddle. You're also going to need strength in your inner and outer thighs to be able to hold your legs open during delivery.

Now here's my other favorite: you'll do the kegel exercises to strengthen the PC muscle so that it can stretch better during the birth. You'll also learn to release the PC so that you can relax it when it comes time to push your baby out. But there are some other excellent reasons you should be giving your PC a workout during these nine months. First, you'll help get rid of that leaky urine problem. Second, you'll be able to make your vaginal canal smaller and put it back into working order after you have your baby. Here's how and why.

You and Your Pelvic Future

Remember I told you to think of the pelvis as a bag of groceries and the pelvic floor as the bottom of the bag. So what's in that bag of groceries? A bowel, a bladder, and a uterus. And as you know, by your ninth month of pregnancy, you have about 13½ pounds—your baby, your uterus, the amniotic fluid, and the placenta—pressing down on your PC every time you stand up. This is a load!

Figure 10
THE PELVIC BASEMENT: Your pelvis is like a bag of groceries. If the bottom of the bag (the pelvic floor) is weak, your groceries (bowel, bladder, and uterus) will fall out.

If you are carrying around a paper bag full of groceries and the bottom of the bag gets wet, your groceries will fall out, right? (See Figure 10.) That's what happens here—weak pelvic floor muscles are like the bottom of a bulging wet paper bag. If you don't strengthen the PC, it becomes a pelvic basement instead of a pelvic floor—and when it goes to the basement, it takes all of the organs with it. I'm not saying your baby is going to fall out, but I am saying you're a good candidate, at some point down the road, for a prolapsed uterus, which occurs when the uterus drops down into the vagina.

Now many women who are heading toward a prolapsed uterus can be helped. How? By strengthening the PC—by doing their kegel exercises, which are named for Dr. Arnold Kegel, who invented them back in 1948. (Although he got only a little publicity at the time, the guy was a genius in his understanding of the function and importance of this critical muscle in a woman's body.) In fact, it is even possible these days to use biofeedback to test the muscle's strength and practice working it. Many women have gained muscle awareness through a unique invention available in some medical facilities—a small probe is inserted into the vagina, you squeeze on it, and the computer tells you how strong your PC is and lets you see what happens when you contract and release it.

A weak PC is correctable. A prolapsed uterus is avoidable. And yet this remains a major cause of surgery on women. Your uterus falls down in your vagina, and what does the doctor do? He comes in, takes his string, and ties the uterus up to something higher. But gravity is always with us! And gravity is going to be pulling on the uterus and the string every time you stand up and walk around. Fail to strengthen the foundation—the PC, the bottom of the bag—and you're always going to have problems, surgery or not. You're going to have everything hanging down between your knees.

Besides supporting your insides, aiding elimination, and being one of the critical birthing muscles, the PC has another function—enhancing sexual enjoyment. The vagina is normally long and narrow, the better to feel your partner's penis and experience the joy of lovemaking. During a vaginal birth, the vagina gets stretched out. As a result, you can't feel your partner's penis as well, and some of the joy goes out of sex.

Once upon a time doctors used to use string to tighten up the opening to the vagina. The result was that penetration became painful while everything behind the string stayed loose. It's muscular. It's all muscular! If you exercise your PC in the way you'll learn here, you will shorten and tighten the muscles around your vaginal canal naturally. And you need to start doing these exercises *now,* during your pregnancy, because in addition to getting them ready for the marathon of labor, it's hard to work the pelvic floor muscles after you've given birth if you've never done so before.

One more thing about sexual appreciation: if you do your pelvic floor exercises during intercourse you will heighten the enjoyable sensations. When you squeeze your PC, your partner will feel a pleasurable tightening around his penis. If your partner squeezes *his* PC during intercourse, his penis will hit the top part of your vagina, sometimes called the G-spot, and that will add to your pleasure. Men, too, have a pubococcygeus muscle. In a man, it forms a figure eight around the opening to the rectum and around the penis.

Now you can see why I sometimes give "Kegel Me, Baby" T-shirts to the husbands of my clients. Couples that kegel together stay together. When you go to sleep at night, count kegels instead of sheep.

Figure 11   PROPER POSTURE DURING PREGNANCY: From the side, good posture can be seen as an imaginary line through the ear, shoulder, hip, knee, and ankle. You can also see the three natural curves in your back.

Waiting It Out, Feeling Good

Now put all this together, and during these 280 days of living in your strange, wonderful, misshapen, exciting pregnant body you will feel more comfortable and more in control of what's going on.

Look back at the typical pregnancy posture we showed you toward the beginning of this chapter. Now look at this picture (see Figure 11) of the way you *should* be standing and carrying yourself—neck straight, chin tucked in, shoulders and chest lifted up and pulled back and buttocks tucked under. As you strengthen and stretch muscles and develop added flexibility where you need it, you'll find it easier to assume and maintain this posture, and that in turn will make everything else that calls for good body mechanics—walking, sitting, getting up—a *whole* lot more pleasant.

And as you practice breathing right and relaxing right, you'll decrease stress, increase stamina and endurance, and, ideally, feel great enough to enjoy the whole nine months.

Right now I want you to remember everything you've learned about breathing, working muscles, and stresses on the body, and let's do a flash-forward to the big day itself, the day your baby is born.

CHAPTER 4

The Big Day

A Preview, Including Everything You Really Wanted to Know About Childbirth but Were Afraid to Ask

Picture this: In a brightly lit room crowded with a lot of machines and people, a pregnant woman, soon to become un-pregnant, lies on a birthing bed. She's in the delivery room at the end of stage two labor; her baby is about ready to get out of there. The woman has been in the hospital for several hours already, mostly lying in bed, where she passed the time puffing and panting through contractions and, as she was advised to do, staring at a spot on the wall trying to distract herself from the painful stuff going on in her body. She was dying for a cup of tea or even a glass of water, but had to content herself with chomping on teeny bits of ice because she wasn't allowed to eat or drink anything.

Now she's on her back with her knees pulled back and her legs wavering and quavering out to the side. Various people—her obstetrician, perhaps a nurse or two, her coach-spouse—are offering instructions each time a new contraction begins: "Okay, here we go. Grab hold of your knees. Hold your breath and push! Hold your breath and push! Push harder! There you go! A little harder!" and so on. The soon-to-be-delivered-of woman is getting very red in the face.

Now the baby's head is crowning—a splendid, transcendent moment for his mother, who may be able to see a part of that little fuzzy skull for the first time by looking into the round mirror positioned near the foot of the bed. Now the doctor turns the mirror around and uses scissors to snip the woman's perineum. The woman does not feel this cut (yet) because that area has become desensitized by the pressure of the baby's head and perhaps by a shot of Novocain. The point of this little snip is to enlarge the opening to the vagina and thus help ease the baby out.

The youngster is born, to everyone's delight, and spends some time lying against his mother as they stare into each other's eyes. Then he's moved off down the hall to the nursery, and she's moved off in another direction to the recovery room. Life begins.

What's wrong with this picture? The birth of a healthy baby, however it happens, is always a grand and glorious thing, a cause for rejoicing. Other than that, just about everything, to my mind, is wrong with this picture! That hardworking woman, at the height of her marathon of labor, isn't getting the kind of help she needs. If all those people would just leave her alone, trust me—she and her body would figure out a better way to get the job done.

Things are changing, and the medical profession is slowly getting more enlightened, but the scene above remains the norm in hospitals in this country. That it does so has to do with certain prevailing myths about women and what goes on when they have babies.

Myth number 1: A woman about to give birth should hold her breath and push. I'm starting with the breathing business, because if you've come with me this far you already know a lot about breathing and you know it's one of the subjects I get fanatical about.

Figure 12 DON'T HOLD YOUR BREATH! The Valsalva maneuver (breath holding) is bad for your health.

Holding your breath and bearing down is called the Valsalva maneuver. This is so bad for you that the American College of Obstetricians and Gynecologists, in its guidelines, says that pregnant women should not do exercises involving the Valsalva maneuver. Why, then, do the majority of delivery room personnel tell you to hold your breath and push? They persist in believing that this is the most effective method for getting the baby out when in fact the Valsalva maneuver is ineffective. Also, in my opinion, it's wrong, it's dangerous, and it leaves you in worse shape afterward than you need to be (see Figure 12). Here's what can happen when you hold your breath and push as long and hard as you can:

1. Your blood pressure may go crazy. When you stop breathing, it increases. Then, as you push and your cardiac output decreases, it goes down. When you stop pushing, your blood pressure goes down some more; then it shoots back up to an even

higher pressure than when you started. That's why we see women after labor with popped blood vessels in their eyes or faces. That's also why these women have an increased possibility of suffering a stroke.

2. You may take in less oxygen and get less of it to your baby, who in turn can suffer fetal distress, including increased levels of blood carbon dioxide from hypoxia, an abnormal condition resulting from a decrease in oxygen supply.

3. Your transverse muscle moves forward. Try it now—put your hand on your belly, hold your breath, and feel the transverse popping frontward. And what's in front of the transverse? The recti. What type of recti? Weakened recti. So when you hold your breath and pop out that transverse, not only does the move interfere with your ability to push back against the uterus, it also pushes the recti out and apart. If you didn't already have a diastasis, you will acquire one during the second stage of labor. And if you had one, it will get bigger.

4. Holding your breath and pushing puts strain on the supporting ligaments of the uterus and bladder.

5. You quickly exhaust yourself if, as those people are shouting at you to do, you push, push, push. Studies show that prolonged bearing down—more than five to seven seconds at a time—*combined with holding one's breath,* is needlessly tiring. And this is not a time you want to run out of steam.

6. Besides all that, if you curl up into a C position at each contraction, hands on your knees as you hold your breath and push, you put enormous strain on your upper back, your shoulders, and your abdominals, which you will feel enormously the next day, just when you want to get used to carrying around your brand-new baby.

If you're a gym habitué, you know that trainers instruct you *not* to hold your breath but to *breathe* while you're doing the work. What physiological sense does it make to hold your breath while you're doing the hardest work you'll ever do in your life? No sense. This advice, in my opinion, is outdated and needs to be changed.

As you do the exercises you'll learn in Chapters 7 and 8, I advise you to keep counting out loud—count the number of seconds you're holding in and strengthening a muscle, for example. The reason: if you're counting, you're exhaling, and if you're exhaling, you're breathing. And that's one of my big messages—keep breathing!

Keep breathing throughout the second stage of labor. It really will feel more naturally right and in sync with what your body wants to do. Your body will tell you when it's time for a push. As you feel that urge to push, take an expanding belly breath to fill your lungs, and then pull your transverse in as you let out a good, vigorous breath. This is sometimes called exhalation pushing, and studies show that for most women it takes no longer to get the baby out this way than by using the dreadful Valsalva maneuver.

Myth number 2: The best place for a woman to deliver a baby is on a bed, lying down. Backtrack to that picture of our childbirthing woman flat on her back on a hospital bed, feet up in stirrups or pulled back toward her head. Again, does this make sense? Does it seem logical? It doesn't and it isn't. I hate the idea of a woman lying on her back to deliver. Here's what's wrong with that position:

1. Gravity is against you. Your 13½ pounds of uterus points upward instead of toward your vagina, through which its contents must emerge. You want what's up to come down and out, and lying on your back obviously does not facilitate that process (more a little later on a better position).

2. It's harder to work the transverse when you're flat on your back—especially when your feet are up in the air. Again, gravity is not on your side at the time when you need to marshal your abdominal strength and get power coming from the center. And the transverse, as you know, is the key birthing muscle, the one you'll use to push your baby out. Even if you're in love with the Tupler Technique and you've been strengthening that transverse throughout your pregnancy, you'll still have a harder time putting it to work if you're lying on your back.

3. Lying flat on your back to deliver does nothing to help your pelvis do its job. A pregnant woman's pelvis is a marvelous piece of machinery, ideally designed to accommodate an emerging baby. Remember that the hormone relaxin has been working on your joints for the last nine months and has made your pelvis very flexible. Your pelvis has actually gotten bigger or opened up throughout your pregnancy in preparation for birth.

    It will open up even more if you are not lying on your back during second stage labor. And that means a decrease in the possibility that you will have your baby by cesarean section, since a leading cause of C-sections is cephalopelvic disproportion, meaning that the mother's pelvic bones aren't opening up enough for the baby's head to get through.

If lying flat in bed is not the best, what position is better as you're getting ready to deliver? Whatever works and is less stressful to you and your baby. You should know—most of us have seen ancient illustrations that depict women in labor—that in non-Western countries throughout the world and throughout the ages, women have given birth in many different ways. They get down on all fours, they sit on birthing chairs, they squat or stand up, holding on to poles or ropes, or they assume other upright positions.

Lying flat on your back is a cultural oddity that's actually a fairly recent phenomenon. According to some historians, Louis XIV of France started this trend. Because he wanted a better look at what was going on, he had his mistresses lie flat on a bed with their legs up in the air when they were about to give birth. And what was good for royalty came to be good enough for everybody else. These days the supine position is more of a convenience for the doctor, who doesn't have to bend over and move around so much, than it is an aid to you.

I'm here to give three cheers for squatting as a comfortable, physiologically sensible position to assume as you go through the second stage of labor—pushing—and get that baby out. It's real easy, and it does great stuff for your abdominals, your back, your buttocks, and your pelvic floor muscles. We'll talk more about this later. And as you'll see when you get to the exercise sections, you will be incorporating squats into your routine throughout the whole nine months.

If you practice squatting while you're pregnant, it won't feel odd or awkward or uncomfortable to squat during contractions when you get to the big day. Even if our cultural prejudices and hospital practices compel you to get up on the delivery table when the baby is actually emerging, you can still squat through earlier labor contractions, with your partner's help, and open up that pelvis and get gravity working for you.

Some hospitals now offer squatting bars, which are attached to the side of the bed or to the wall. The woman can hold this bar to ease herself down into a supported squat. You can also purchase a squatting stool and bring it with you to the hospital. Information is listed in Resources, at the back of this book.

These aids are not yet available in most hospitals, but I have no doubt that as they become more widely available, women will gratefully take advantage of them. Some delivery rooms nowadays do have birthing beds, in which the woman sits up with her back supported—again, much less stressful than the *supine* position, but also again, not yet terribly common.

There are various ways to delivery: squat on the bed with your coaches holding you on either side or assume a semi-squat while standing up, with your partner supporting you under the arms from behind. Try this and see how it feels. Studies in England of women who delivered using the birth cushion and women who gave birth lying flat on their backs concluded that the women who were squatting pushed for thirty-five minutes, while the supine women had to push for forty-five minutes. Also,

9 percent of the squatters required a forceps delivery, compared with 16 percent of the non-squatters. This position works!

Myth number 3: A woman needs some surgical assistance to get the baby out. That doctor who took his scissors and snipped open our birthing woman's perineum was performing an episiotomy, a procedure done on more than three-quarters of first-time mothers in this country. The medical profession's reasoning goes like this: the baby's emerging head might tear the perineum; therefore we'll cut you first so you won't tear, and a straight cut will heal better than a jagged tear.

To start with, this is faulty reasoning. What happens when you cut a slit in the side of a piece of fabric? It can still tear, right? In fact, it will tend to tear more easily. So cutting you doesn't stop you from tearing. If you tear, the opening will have jagged edges, and yes, those are harder for the doctor to sew up, but in fact, zigzag edges naturally close and heal more effectively.

Here's another fact: a large-scale study conducted at McGill University in Canada concluded that women who do not undergo episiotomies *have less birth trauma and recover more quickly*. The researchers said:

• Episiotomies conferred no benefit in the prevention of injury to the birth canal tissue.
• All women—episiotomy or no—delivered healthy babies.
• The women with episiotomies had larger tears than those who tore naturally, and they also reported more pain and healed more slowly.
• Women who got through childbirth without either a natural tear or an episiotomy felt great.

Therefore, said these researchers, "it is our recommendation that liberal or routine use of episiotomy be abandoned." The American College of Obstetricians and Gynecologists agrees. ACOG's guidelines state that episiotomies should not be routinely used in untroubled births.

Does this surprise you? Of course not. Women who have had these little snips tell me it's the worst thing about the birth! First of all, getting sewn up hurts! Then, when you want to enjoy your new baby and get up and move around, you *still* hurt. You can't sit comfortably; you can't cough or sneeze or have a bowel movement comfortably; you have a wound in an area of you body that is naturally moist and not exposed to much air, so healing occurs slowly. Is it any wonder some people are now calling the episiotomy the Western method of genital mutilation?

Most women don't need an episiotomy. I've had clients who delivered big, fat ten-pound babies without experiencing tears or cuts. Midwives regularly practice marvelous, kind, humane methods—warm packs and oil and massage—to soften and stretch the perineum. They're gentle with that area because they're women, and they know how much it can hurt to sustain a wound there.

If throughout your pregnancy you've been doing your kegel exercises—we'll show you how in the BAKS Basics (Chapter 7)—and if you've strengthened your pelvic floor muscles and practiced relaxing them, you'll be supple and in control of these muscles when the big day comes, and unless something unforeseen crops up, you won't need an episiotomy even if you're giving birth to a little Attila the Hun! (Again, here's why a sitting or squatting position during delivery is to be preferred. Lying flat on your back is hard on the perineal area.)

Myth number 4: A woman in labor must not eat or drink. This idea got started only about fifty years ago when general anesthesia was routinely administered during childbirth. It was believed that a woman with a full stomach had a greater chance of developing postanesthetic pneumonia from vomiting and having the stomach contents enter her lungs (pulmonary aspiration). So a firm rule was established: nothing by mouth for you even if your tongue feels like cardboard and you know a cup of bouillon would warm and comfort you.

In fact, pulmonary aspiration has been shown to be related to the type of anesthesia and its management, not to how recently or how much a woman has ingested. Very few women these days, in any case, receive general anesthesia. So why persist with the unsupported, outdated practice of fasting during labor?

Studies show that laboring women who are allowed to eat and drink what they want can regulate themselves very nicely. The great majority want something light to eat during the early stages of labor. All want something to drink. In one study, conducted in Great Britain, women who monitored their own food and liquid intake had shorter labor and required less pain relief than those who didn't.

Women getting ready to give birth know what they need. *You* will know what you need. If you need a glass of water, you should be able to have a glass of water.

Myth number 5: A woman can't have a baby without a bunch of people telling her when to push. One of my clients told me she found the urgings of her delivery room companions intensely irritating at a time when she was totally focused on her body and its sensations and signals: "I wanted them all to just shut up and get out of my face, including my husband." I've heard words to that effect from many, many women.

Surely one of the great positive developments in how we give birth has been the welcoming, or at least the tolerating, of husbands, partners, or loved ones. Most of them want to be with us during this difficult, spectacular process, and we want them to be with us, not pacing around in some bleak waiting room down the hall.

But our loving helpmates can get carried away with their coaching roles, and believe me, nobody's going to need to tell you when to push. Your body will tell you, because you're the one doing the job. I see a similarity here to people telling you that you ought to focus on a spot on the wall to distract yourself during contraction peaks. If you find it a helpful trick, by all means use it, but it's an unnatural idea. Can you imagine an animal deciding: I'm in pain, let me stare at something? If you'd rather squeeze your eyes shut and grunt and groan, you should do so.

Get your husband or partner to read this book, or at least explain to him or her its principles. The support person who'll be with you on the big day may serve his or her highest purpose by fighting off the doctors or nurses who are telling you to hold your breath and push, or by seeing to it that your wishes are respected in other ways. In other words, use your partner not only as your support person but also as your advocate.

Despite all this, we really have come a long way, baby, from those days when childbirth and the nine months leading up to it were considered and treated as sort of a benign illness. Many of the places where women give birth are now warm and pleasant and actively designed to enable a normal process to take place in a normal atmosphere—lights aren't blinding, nice pictures hang on the walls, people can walk around and talk and even have something to eat if they want.

But there's a way to go. Here are some comments from the Committee on Health and Regulation of the National Women's Health Network, a nonprofit coalition of four hundred women's health groups, individual consumers, and health providers: "American parents are becoming increasingly aware that well-intentioned health professionals do not always have scientific data to support common American obstetrical practices and that many of these practices are carried out primarily because they are part of medical and hospital tradition."

And this: "The pregnant patient has the right to participate in decisions involving her well-being and that of her unborn child, unless there is a clear-cut medical emergency that prevents her participation."

The more you prepare your body and inform your brain during your pregnancy, the more in control you will be of what goes on when your baby is born. And the more you talk things over beforehand with the other people who will be there on the big day, the better your chances will be of getting the most comfortable, most low-stress labor and delivery.

Raul Artal is a fellow of the American College of Obstetricians and Gynecologists and the American College of Sports Medicine. He has a dual professorship in obstetrics and gynecology and exercise science at the University of Southern California and helped to develop the exercise guidelines of ACOG. Artal strongly supports the notion that a pregnant woman should be provided with all the facts concerning her pregnancy so that she can make the final decisions (she may also choose to consult her partner). An obstetrician, who has access to a wide selection of technological and medical information, should play the role of helper, adviser, and teacher; as a medical professional, he or she will work toward the healthiest possible outcome for both mother and baby and will provide support and guidance, including medical intervention if it is required. But ultimately, Artal states, "It's the woman herself who now plays the leading role and is the star of the show!"

Sounding Out Your Doctor

If you will be delivering your baby in a hospital or birthing center with your obstetrician or family doctor in attendance, have a talk with him or her well before your due date about what to expect when you arrive at the hospital or center. Many pregnant women, I've discovered, feel somewhat diffident or reluctant about asking questions or stating their own preferences. Remember, this will be your big day, and it's perfectly appropriate for you to raise the issues that concern you ahead of time. Here are some questions you may want to ask your doctor:

- During the first stage of labor I would like to be able to walk around if I feel like it and to assume a squatting position during contractions. Does the nursing staff generally encourage this kind of activity? If not, what can we do to make my wishes known?

- What is your feeling about episiotomies? How regularly do you perform an episiotomy? I would prefer not to have this surgery unless it's absolutely necessary. Is there anything you can do to help prevent my having an episiotomy?

- What kind of pain medication might be administered? In particular, I'd like to know about the availability and efficacy of the short-acting epidural so I can use my legs while pushing.

- I believe it will be more difficult for me to deliver if I'm lying on my back than if I am in a more upright position. Will a birthing stool or some other aid be available for me to use? If not, can I bring something? I might like to squat or sit up during delivery. Will this be a problem?

- We'd like to bring along some herbal tea and crackers in case I want a snack. Is there any policy at the hospital concerning eating during labor? Do I have to have an I.V.?

- We also plan to bring a small battery-powered tape recorder, so I can listen to music before and during delivery. Will this be a problem?

- Can I have a professional labor support person, besides my partner, with me during delivery?

- I have been practicing certain breathing and pushing techniques as well as strengthening my abdominal muscles during pregnancy, in preparation for childbirth. They may be different from the usual advice of holding your breath, but can I count on your support?

CHAPTER 5

Before You Begin

Do's and Don'ts, and Other Stuff to Know About Pregnancy and Exercise

During the dark old days when having a baby was considered akin to being sick, pregnant women weren't supposed to exercise. Now we know better, and the American College of Obstetricians and Gynecologists has given its stamp of approval to exercise during pregnancy and the postpartum period. "In the absence of either obstetric or medical complications," says the *ACOG Bulletin,* "pregnant women can continue to exercise and derive related benefits." And: "Women who have achieved cardiovascular fitness prior to pregnancy should be able to safely maintain that level of fitness throughout pregnancy and the postpartum period."

So if you listen to what your body is telling you and you apply yourself to the exercises we'll show you later, you'll be fine. You will be more than fine; you will be shaping up for the marathon of labor.

Here are some do's and don'ts to help you prepare yourself:

Do get your doctor's okay before beginning any exercise program, including the Maternal Fitness routine, and before continuing any exercising you were doing before you became pregnant. He or she should be able to discuss with you any medical circumstances, relating either to your pregnancy or to your general health, that might have an impact on your working out. Certain specific conditions, such as chronic hypertension, active thyroid, cardiac, vascular, or pulmonary disease, may require some women to modify their exercise programs or to avoid exercise altogether.

According to ACOG guidelines, if you have any of the following obstetric conditions, you should not exercise during your pregnancy:

- Pregnancy-induced hypertension
- Pre-term rupture of membranes (rupture of the amniotic sac and leaking of amniotic fluid)
- Pre-term labor during a prior or the current pregnancy or both
- Incompetent cervix cerclage (the procedure by which the cervix is stitched closed after conception as an aid in maintaining the pregnancy)
- Persistent second- or third-trimester bleeding
- Intrauterine growth retardation (inadequate development of the fetus or placenta)

Many women who miscarried previously wonder if they should avoid exercising during their current pregnancies. Those of my clients who have had prior miscarriages proceed comfortably and effectively through the Maternal Fitness program. If you have had a miscarriage, wait out the first trimester and get started slowly in your second trimester with the BAKS Basics (the beginning exercises I'll show you in Chapter 7). And *always* discuss your plans with your doctor.

Do dress comfortably while you exercise. Wear sweatpants and a top or other loose clothing. You want to keep that air circulation through your clothes, so if you work up a little sweat it will evaporate and cool you down. A supportive maternity bra will help prevent unnecessary stretching of breast tissue.

And wear properly fitting athletic shoes to support the softened ligaments and tendons in your feet.

Do supply yourself with two pieces of equipment. First, invest in an exercise mat. These inexpensive items are available in sporting goods shops and are necessary to protect your knees and hands during the on-all-fours exercises we'll be doing. Working on a mat will also cushion your back during routines where you will be supine. A nice thick rug with good padding underneath it will do the trick too, but I think you'll be more comfortable if you work on a mat.

Second, buy a Dyna-Band. This little brightly colored strip of stretchy rubber is one of the greatest inventions since sliced bread. Several of the exercises in the routine you'll learn in Chapter 8 call for using a Dyna-Band, and as soon as you start working with one you'll notice how much it will benefit you. Doing body moves against the resistance of this giant rubber band really works those muscles. Select the proper level of resistance when you purchase your Dyna-Band: beginning, intermediate, or advanced. Do slow, controlled movements so that the work does not put extra stress on relaxed joints, and maintain a firm grip on the band so that it does not snap out of your hands. Check the Resources section at the end of this book to find out how to order the Dyna-Band.

There's a third piece of equipment you might want to consider. If you've been working with handheld weights, you can keep doing so in several of the exercises we'll show you. If you haven't yet used weights but want to give them a try, start modestly. ACOG recommends using light weights (2 to 5 pounds) and doing weight-lifting moves at least twice a week, with at least twenty-four hours between sessions.

Do begin each workout with a warm-up. You'll see when you start the Maternal Fitness routine described in Chapter 8 that I put you through a series of gentle stretches from your head to your feet, to get the kinks out and warm up your muscles before you put them to work. This is the way to prevent strains, joint injuries, and muscle cramping.

Do begin and end each exercise with a belly breath. Take in a big, lung-filling breath of air through your nose by expanding your belly. Then let out a big, lung-emptying exhalation through your mouth. Suck that transverse back in on the exhalation. Just remember this for now; when we get into the routine, you'll see how it all comes together.

Do count out loud as you do repetitions during the exercises. I'll keep reminding you of this as we go along, but I want to reiterate a simple point: If you're counting, you're exhaling, and if you're exhaling, you're breathing. Breathing is good! If you don't count, you're probably holding your breath, and that's not good.

When you hold your breath, reflex tightening of the pelvic floor may also occur. The kind of breathing you'll be doing as you count off repetitions, however, isn't quite the same as the big belly breath. You'll be holding in your transverse as you're counting and doing the work of the exercise, so you're not going to be sucking in the same large amount of air. Don't worry about it. Just count and breathe, breathe and count.

Do remember to use your transverse abdominal muscle on the work part of your stretching and strengthening exercises.

Do perform the exercises with your eyes closed as much as possible—but not, of course, if you feel you're in danger of losing your balance. Why close your eyes? To shut out visual distractions and to help you focus on the muscles you're working and the way you want them to move. When you close your eyes, that mind-body connection I'm always talking about gets stronger.

Don't lie on your back for too long. What's too long? Some experts say pregnant women should avoid exercising on their backs altogether after the first trimester. But in my opinion, you don't have to be quite that cautious.

For some of the exercises in the routine, I'll ask you to lie on your back, and a minute or two in that position isn't going to hurt you. Just remember that *if you feel light-headed or dizzy, roll over onto your side.* Dizziness happens when your uterus rests on your vena cava, one of the main blood vessels from the heart, decreasing the blood flow to your brain. Rolling onto your side will shift the uterus off the vena cava and clear up the dizziness. Tune in to your body and modify your movements and positions as warranted.

Do sit during exercises you can perform while either sitting or standing. Take a load off your feet. Remember you have more blood in your body these days, and when you're on your feet, a lot of it is going to be pooling in your legs. So why do stuff standing up when you could be sitting down? Why increase your chances of getting varicose veins *and* stressing out your lower back?

Do eat before exercising. If you work out on an empty stomach your body is going to get the energy it needs by burning up body fat, and that's not what you want right now. Remember that during pregnancy *you're not exercising for weight control.*

Work out two to three hours after a meal. If it's been longer than that since you had your last meal, eat a wholesome snack sometime within the hour before you do your exercising. Melon or some other fruit, raisins, and whole wheat crackers are fine munchies because they give good energy without too much wear on the digestive system. Avoid dairy products—they'll increase your chances of developing heartburn during the workout.

Don't exercise if the weather is very hot and humid and you're not in a cool place, and don't exercise if you're feeling flu-ish and running a fever. What's most important here is that you don't want to get overheated.

As you know, your inner core body temperature is already higher than usual, just by virtue of the fact that you're pregnant. You do *not* want to increase your temperature above 101°F. (38°C.), because your baby has no mechanisms for cooling down, such as perspiring or breathing. So avoid exercise if it's really hot or if you're under the weather. For the same reason, avoid saunas, hot tubs, and hot baths.

Swimming, however, is a great exercise when you're pregnant (see Figure 13). You have less chance of getting overheated, and swimming provides an excellent overall muscle and aerobic workout. The breaststroke, in particular, is a fine swimming move because it lengthens the chest muscles, shortens the back muscles, and works your inner and outer leg muscles. If you use a snorkel, you won't have to lift your head up and down out of the water to breathe. That's easier on your neck and takes the stress out of trying to take in air.

The Maternal Fitness program isn't going to get you overheated. If you're involved in other regular exercise regimens and you want to make sure that you're not doing too much too fast in those, take your temperature—the rectal method is considered the most accurate (rectally, your temperature should register 99.6°F.)—after you finish a workout. The reading should not exceed 101°F. (38°C.) If it does, you need to moderate your workout—go slower and work at a lower intensity.

Do drink water before, during, and after any exercising. Keep sipping that water, because exercising can cause you to get dehydrated, and that can increase your body temperature or decrease the amount of your amniotic fluid.

Don't push yourself. If you're like most pregnant women, you'll have high-energy days and low-energy days. On a low day, lighten up your workout by doing fewer repetitions, or do only those exercises that you find easy. Listen to your body, go at your own pace, give yourself rest breaks. And never let yourself get exhausted.

Do be conscious of your huffing and puffing! Here's why: if you're huffing and puffing while doing any kind of aerobic or muscle-strengthening exercises, including our routine, you're doing too much or going too fast, and your heart rate is too high.

You know that aerobic exercise conditions the heart and lungs by increasing the efficiency of the body's oxygen intake. Walking and swimming, for example, are great aerobic exercises. And the good news about aerobic exercise during pregnancy is that researchers have finally put to rest the notion that an exercising woman is taking blood away from the fetus.

Our routine is not a high-intensity aerobic workout—we're concentrating on stretching and strengthening muscles—but you will be exerting yourself and taking in a lot of oxygen, and you should monitor yourself to be sure that you're not overdoing it. Just listen to your body. And specifically, listen for huffing and puffing.

Figure 13 BREAST STROKE:
Doing the breast stroke while using a snorkel is a great exercise, and it's fun to do.

Figure 14 JACKKNIFE:
Getting up this way can make the separation of your abdominal muscles larger.

An easy way to monitor yourself is to use the concept of *perceived exertion*. This means that you should be able to carry on a conversation while you're exercising. If you can't talk comfortably and you're out of breath and huffing, your body is telling you to slow down. Do so!

ACOG advises that the strenuous portion of any exercise routine should not exceed fifteen to twenty minutes; lower-intensity aerobic activities may be conducted for as long as forty-five minutes. The routine we'll be teaching you in Chapter 8 should not get you into any difficulties in this regard.

Do get up the right way after lying down or sitting. Before you were pregnant, you could probably pop right up out of a chair or jackknife (see Figure 14) yourself out of bed in the morning, although even when you're not pregnant, that's not the best way to get up. Now that you've got that belly in front, getting upright is harder. It's also more important to do it right—without letting your abdominals bulge out.

So here's how:

- To get up from a chair, put your hands above your knees, take a belly breath, and bring your transverse in (more about that later). Lean forward and push yourself up with your arms. Finally, roll your spine up one vertebra at a time.
- To go from a sitting position to lying down on your back, roll over onto one hip and use your arms to lower yourself down. Then roll onto your back.
- To sit up from a supine position, roll to one side without lifting your head. Then push yourself up with your hands, letting your head come up last.

I'm going to be repeating this advice later. In addition, when you get started on the routine I'll show you the best way to get up after sitting or lying down. This is important stuff, and the goal is always the same: to prevent the transverse from pressing out against your already weakened rectus abdominis.

Do be aware that while you're pregnant you're somewhat more than normally susceptible to certain exercise reactions. By no means are you bound to get one of these pains while working out, and none of them indicate any danger to you or your baby. Just be conscious of the following reactions, and know how to avoid them and what to do if you experience them:

- *Round ligament pain.* Two round ligaments hold your uterus forward. As the uterus grows bigger, these ligaments get stretched. And this means that you might feel a shooting pain in the groin area if you stand up quickly. If you rest, it will go away. To avoid round ligament pain, get upright slowly, in the way I just described.
- *Leg cramps.* You can get a cramp in your calf while you're exercising, or even in the middle of the night while you're sleeping. Whenever this happens, flex your foot and the cramp should go away. If you're getting a lot of leg cramps, talk to your doctor. You may need more calcium or salt in your diet. (Pregnancy is one time *not* to restrict your salt intake; you'll learn more about this later.)
- *Pubic pain.* The hormone relaxin, as you know, is loosening up your joints, including the symphysis pubic, the line where the two halves of the pubic bone come together. Discontinue any exercise that causes pain in the pubic area. Women who use a StairMaster are especially susceptible to this reaction.
- *Sciatica.* This is another kind of leg pain, caused by irritation of the long sciatic nerve running down the back of the thigh. Pregnant women, because of postural and hormonal changes, are especially susceptible. If you experience sciatica while you're lying on your back—that's when it's most likely to hit—bend the affected leg at the knee, keeping the other leg straight, and relieve the discomfort by gently pulling that sore leg across your body.

Don't do crossovers (see Figure 15) or roll-backs (see Figure 16) while you're pregnant. If you don't know what those are that's fine. They are not part of my routine, but I'm showing illustrations of these moves here because they are included in many popular workouts. Skip them for now. They'll make your diastasis bigger.

Do perform the Maternal Fitness routine regularly. Don't go overboard with your workouts, but don't do them once or twice a week and then forget about them. Ideally and at the very minimum, I suggest you do the BAKS Basics (Chapter 7) every day as a routine, or better yet, incorporate the moves into your everyday activities—

Figure 15 CROSSOVER: *Don't* do this sideward movement during pregnancy. It will push your transverse against the weakened recti.

Figure 16 ROLL-BACK: *Don't* go straight down when getting into a back-lying position. It can increase a diastasis.

while you're riding the bus to work, sitting in a meeting, standing at the kitchen sink, watching TV. Once you become familiar with the exercises, you'll see how easy it is to do them throughout the day.

Do the Maternal Fitness routine (Chapter 8), which incorporates BAKS moves, three times a week. On the days that you don't do the routine, do the BAKS basics.

A reminder: do the BAKS Basics for at least one full week before you embark on the Maternal Fitness routine.

If you have, prior to getting pregnant, been involved in another exercise program, participated in sports, or worked with a personal trainer, and you wish to continue some of that activity, learning the Maternal Fitness routine will be enormously helpful. You'll learn how to modify your other workout to accommodate your pregnancy. If your class is doing an exercise you can't do, sit it out and so some transverse work instead. And, of course, you will learn to include the belly breath–transverse movement in all your other work.

ACOG recommends regular exercise three times a week instead of sporadic activity, as do most experts. Going at your exercises in an on-again, off-again way is more stressful to your body than if you maintain a steady schedule.

All these do's and don'ts apply to any kind of specific exercising you're doing during the whole nine months of your pregnancy. At the same time—as you know better than anyone—your body keeps changing during those months. Early in the game, while you're still trim enough to slip into your twenty-six-inch-waist skirts, you might also be feeling very sick and too pooped to lift a pencil. Later, when you've got your second wind and feel like a powerhouse of a woman, you have that basketball-sized belly getting in your way and making the thought of moving around—much less exercising—unappealing.

Here's a trimester-by-trimester thumbnail sketch of how the way you're feeling and looking might influence how you work the Maternal Fitness routine:

The first trimester. Ninety percent of my clients don't feel like working out during the first three months. They're tired, they're nauseated. Some of them are getting headaches or feeling light-headed or dizzy.

Just rest. Let your body adjust to the remarkable and stressful changes that are overtaking it. If you're in that 90 percent category that doesn't feel well, limit yourself to doing some simple parts of the BAKS Basics—a little transverse work and some kegels while you're lying in bed on your side.

The BAKS works wonderfully during the first trimester, because it's simple stuff. I've used it with women on bed rest, and it's been very successful. You start developing a little muscle strength, but in a low-key, low-stress way that doesn't call for a lot of moving around or changing positions. Especially if you were a fairly sedentary, non-exercising type before you got pregnant, limit yourself to the BAKS. If, on the other hand, you're one of the lucky few who are sailing through these months feeling perfectly fine, do your BAKS and get into the full routine whenever you want.

The second trimester. Most of my clients—you too, probably—feel great during the second trimester. They're not feeling sick to their stomachs all the time, they can breathe comfortably, and they're not yet so big and bulky that it's hard to do things.

If you've been easing into the BAKS Basics during the first trimester and now you're raring to go, increase the intensity of your workout gradually. I want you to do the full BAKS for at least seven days before you get started on the Maternal Fitness routine.

The third trimester. Okay, now you're feeling huge, and that means, for one thing, that working the transverse will be harder. If you've been doing your BAKS abdominal exercises from the start and pulling in that transverse as you work the routine, you've got the feel of how the movement goes, and that will carry you though.

You may be having swelling, so you don't want to do a lot of standing. Our sitting and side-lying exercises are going to feel most comfortable and are best for you.

It's going to be harder to squat during these months. You'll have to open your legs wider to allow room for your belly, but don't give up on your supported squats (more on these in Chapters 7 and 8).

Almost certainly you're going to start feeling fatigued again, as you carry around added weight and, as happens with many of my clients, your growing, active baby will often be keeping you awake at night! Do remember one of our don'ts: don't let yourself get anywhere near a point of exhaustion when you're doing the exercises.

A word about you and your postpartum body: after your baby is born, I want you to keep doing kegels and transverse exercises. This will help you get back your flat abdominals and your tightened vagina, and it will prevent your insides from dropping out at some point in the future.

But postpartum pelvic floor and abdominal work is going to feel very different, because you're stretched out and loose in these areas. In a sense, you'll have to do this work by rote memory as the muscles return to their pre-pregnancy state. If you keep working them while you're pregnant, you'll have the mind-body awareness that will enable you to exercise effectively afterward.

And there's an added incentive: we've found that women who are diligent about doing their abdominal work during the nine months of pregnancy are less likely to get stretch marks! This makes sense. Bring in the transverse and you bring in your skin along with it.

CHAPTER 6

A Do-It-Yourself Fitness Evaluation

How Do You Measure Up in Terms of Posture, Muscle Strength, and Flexibility?

As I said in the last chapter, do discuss your exercise plans with your doctor before you get started. He or she will be monitoring all the medical vitals during your pregnancy and will be able to let you know if any special conditions make working out inadvisable. Chances are, that's not going to be the case.

What doctors probably *aren't* going to do is talk to you about your bones, joints, posture, muscles, and lifestyle—and what all of that has to do with exercising your pregnant body.

When a client first comes to my Maternal Fitness studio, one of my trainers or I will put her through a short and painless evaluation that gives us information about her pre-pregnancy status: what kind of exercise, if any, she was doing before her pregnancy, and what she's doing now; which muscles are stronger and which are weaker; what kind of job she has (is she sitting all day); and how flexible she is. I put all the pieces together to come up with a kind of fitness profile that will let us individualize the workout. One woman might need to pay special attention to upper back work, go lighter on the weights she's been using, or not do too much squatting.

I want this book to feel and work as if you have me right in your living room, so I'm going to show you how to do your own at-home version of my evaluation and come up with your own fitness profile. And as we go along, I'll offer some suggestions on how you might want to adjust the exercises you're going to start doing as you work your way through the next two chapters. So let's start with a few easy questions and a few simple tests.

How's your posture? From the side, good posture can be seen as an imaginary vertical line running down the body through the ear, shoulder, hip, knee, and ankle. Here's how to see if yours is properly aligned: Stand with your back against a wall, heels against the wall. Stand straight, but normally—don't throw your head or shoulders back. Check yourself or, even better, ask your spouse or partner to do so, in the following ways:

- Is your neck erect, chin in, and head in balance directly above your shoulders? That's good. Are your neck and shoulders markedly forward and your chin markedly jutting out? That needs work.
- Is your upper back straight or only nominally rounded? That's good. Is your upper back markedly rounded? That needs work.
- Do you have lots of room around the curve of your lower spine? Put your hand back there and feel how much space there is between you and the wall. If there is room to accommodate anything bigger than your fist, that needs work.
- Are your feet pointing straight ahead? That's good. Are they markedly pointing out, with your ankles sagging in a little? That needs work.

If it's still very early in your pregnancy and you're coming up on the "needs work" end posture-wise, all this neck, shoulder, and back stuff is going to get more pronounced as the pregnancy progresses and your growing belly and breasts start pulling everything forward. Be religious about doing your BAKS Basics (Chapter 7), and you'll see how your posture will improve.

Do you have any problem areas? Have you in the past had any broken bones, fractures, serious sprains? Any chronic problems in the back, knees, wrists, or shoulders? If so, pregnancy can exacerbate those problems or areas of weakness, because of postural changes and increased joint laxity. Keep this advice in mind.

- If you have a *weak back,* you'll want to modify some of the exercises slightly. In general when working out:

1. Be very careful about getting yourself up and down the right way, as you learned in the do's and don'ts. When getting up from a sitting position on the floor, move onto all fours, then move into the hands-above-the-knees position and push upright with your arms.

2. Make sure your back is always flat, supported, and in the recommended position.

3. Keeping that transverse in at fifth floor (see page 69) is crucial, because that's what supports the lower back as you do your moves.

If you have *knee problems*—weakness in the joint, some discomfort when bending at the knees—here's what you should remember:

1. Be very careful that your knee is in the recommended position during each of the exercises.

2. I recommend *not* doing forward or side lunges while you're pregnant. My routine does not include lunges, but they are part of many popular workouts.

3. Again, be very conscientious about getting up and down the right way, as you've learned.

4. When leaving the squatting position, don't stand up directly. Sit first, easing yourself down and back with your arms. Then get onto all fours, place your hands above your knees, and rise.

If you have *weak wrists,* you'll feel more comfortable during on-all-fours exercises if you are resting on your closed fists rather than on flattened palms.

Think about which areas of your body, if any—from the previous injury or natural predisposition—might tend to be vulnerable, and then make the small modifications I'll show you that will prevent discomfort or added stress. If you have had problems with your shoulders, be careful doing any upper body exercises that involve lifting your arms over your head, especially while holding weights.

How flexible are you? Actually, we want to find out if you are super flexible. And that's what you are if you can do the following moves:

• Sitting on the floor with your legs spread apart, you can bend forward at the waist, keeping your back flat, and touch your chest to the floor. (This, of course, is before you got pregnant or very early in your pregnancy, before your belly gets in the way.)

• Sitting on the floor with your legs together, you can reach forward and extend your hands past your toes.

• Sitting with your arms raised out to the sides at shoulder level and bent at the elbows, you can bring your elbows way back behind your shoulders.

• Squatting with your weight on the outer edges of your feet, you can keep your heels on the floor and comfortably hold the squat for a minute or more.

If you *can* do all that—especially the first one—you are super flexible—perhaps because you were born that way or perhaps as a result of prior exercise, dance, gymnastics, or other forms of athletics. The thing to be aware of now is that pregnancy is going to make you even more flexible because of that hormone-produced joint laxity. And that's going to make you more prone to injury during exercise. Very flexible people tend to thrash around; their movements are broader and larger than they intend them to be, and that can mean strains, sprains, or tears in the joints, muscles, or ligaments.

If you are one of these super flexible people, here are the two most important rules to remember when you're doing the workout:

1. Do not *over*stretch in the stretching exercises.
2. Be conscious always of keeping your movements slow and controlled.

How strong are your muscles? In particular, it will be useful for you to get an idea of your lower-body strength before you start to exercise: how strong are the muscles in your thighs and in your pelvic floor? Those muscles are most important during labor and delivery, and we will be working them in the BAKS Basics and the routine.

To evaluate the muscle strength in your outer and inner thighs, get your spouse or partner to help you as follows:

• *Abductor (outer thigh) check.* Sit with your back supported against the wall, feet on the floor, legs bent at the knees, knees about twelve inches apart, hands resting on thighs. Have your partner put his hands on your outer thighs just above your knees. Push your knees out to the sides as your partner offers resistance to your push. The easier it is for you to move against that resistance, the stronger your outer thigh muscles are.

• *Adductor (inner thigh) check.* Starting in the same position as for the outer thigh check, have your partner put his hands on your inner thighs, just above your knees. Try to bring your knees together as your partner offers resistance. The easier it is for you to move against that resistance, the stronger your inner thigh muscles are.

If you're not starting out with a great deal of strength in your thigh muscles, the leg lifts you will do in our routine will be of enormous benefit. Walking and most other aerobic exercises will strengthen the fronts and backs of your legs, but they won't do much for your inner and outer leg muscles. And those are the ones you need to avoid the pregnancy waddle and to enable you to hold the positions of labor.

• *Pelvic floor check.* Remember how to contract your pelvic floor muscles? Pretend you're urinating and then squeeze in the muscle that will stop the flow of urine. In a sitting position with your legs apart and your abdominals relaxed, do that now as you count to ten and hold in the muscle.

If you can hold the muscle in for ten seconds, your pelvic floor muscles are fairly strong. If you can hold the muscle in for only two or three counts without it wavering, it needs strengthening.

When you start doing kegels—pelvic floor muscle squeezes—in the BAKS Basics, you'll have to begin slowly if you don't have a lot of strength in this area. Do your kegels from the easiest position and hold the squeeze for five counts instead of ten. The "elevator exercise" you'll learn will be a good indication of your developing muscle strength.

Are you a fitness enthusiast? You're into sports. You walk upstairs instead of taking the elevator. You belong to a gym, and you work out on the machines. You take a couple of aerobics classes a week. You can name your muscles. Regular exercise and feeling fit are a big part of your life.

So probably you generally have good muscle tone, good cardiovascular strength, and a lot of stamina. Pregnancy is going to change some of that. ACOG mentions a study of women who were very active prior to becoming pregnant—runners, aerobic dancers, and cross-country skiers. Of these women, 60 percent reported significantly decreased exercise performance during the early months of pregnancy, and only one out of ten kept going at near preconception levels throughout pregnancy.

Hardly a surprise, right? You're dealing with first-trimester fatigue and maybe nausea, with added weight and a radical shift in your center of gravity, and although you've always walked upstairs effortlessly, suddenly you're getting winded because it's harder to breathe. Here's what you should remember as you get into the routine:

1. Get really good with those belly breaths. That's how you'll get enough oxygen to fill up your well-conditioned lungs.
2. If you have been doing exercises with weights, reduce the amount you're lifting. If you've been working with ten-pound dumbbells, for example, you might want to switch to five-pound weights. Because of the joint laxity of pregnancy, it's wise to err on the side of safety and decrease the weight you may have been used to.
3. Know that even if you are familiar with some of the stretches and other movements we'll be doing, they're going to be harder now because you will be coordinating them with working the transverse. Adding in the transverse will be a different way of working out for you, and it's going to take concentration.

Are you a couch potato? The last time you got any regular exercise was back in school, when phys ed was a required course. You've never owned a Lycra workout suit. It's fine by you if you never work up a sweat.

Our program is going to do wonders for you, but here are some things to remember:

1. Start slowly. Instead of doing the BAKS Basics for seven days before getting into the full routine, you might want to spend two weeks on the BAKS alone.

2. If you're a non-exerciser *and* your job involves sitting at a desk all day, very likely you do not have good upper body strength. Your chest muscles are shortened, your upper back muscles are stretched out, your shoulders are rounded, and as you know, all this is going to be exaggerated as your pregnancy progresses. The pectoral stretches we'll be doing are going to be great for you, but take it easy when you first get started. Those muscles have been just sitting there, and it will take time to get them where they should be.

3. I'm guessing you've never used a Dyna-Band before. Work very slowly with the Dyna-Band until you get a feel for it. As I said in Chapter 5, be sure to select the proper level of resistance when you purchase the band. If you have never worked with one before, I suggest you use the beginner level. As you get stronger, you can always increase the resistance yourself by working with a shorter length of band.

4. If you've never used weights, skip them until you're absolutely comfortable doing the movement of a particular exercise, including the transverse. Especially for non-exercisers, it's hard to work that transverse that you're used to not

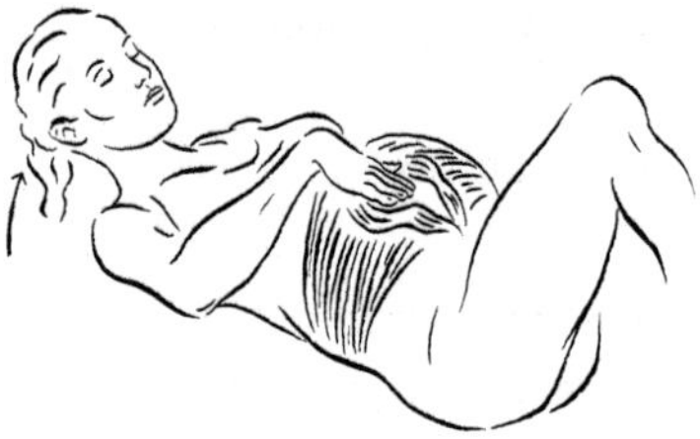

Figure 17　Diastasis
Check:
Lie on your back with
your knees bent; put
your fingers (pointing
down) over your navel
and press down gently
as you lift your head.

working, and to coordinate that with upper body or leg moves. It's like trying to pat your head and rub your belly at the same time.

5. Do fewer repetitions or sets, and work your way up as you get stronger. Listen to your body.

Do you have a diastasis? Many pregnant women get this separation of the two halves of the rectus abdominis muscle. Check yourself by lying on your back with your knees bent. With your fingers pointing toward your feet, hold your hand flat on your belly right on the belly button (see Figure 17). Lift your head as high as you can—the higher you lift your head, the easier it will be to feel the muscle—and see if you feel a separation in the muscle under your hand. If you have a separation, you will feel and see a ridge protruding out from the midline of your abdomen—this is a diastasis. Check in the same way a bit above and below your belly button; in some women, a diastasis may extend the length of the muscle.

A diastasis is not harmful to you or your baby, and is a way of protecting your abdominals from overstretching. But a diastasis does mean a temporarily weakened abdomen and less support for your back.

If you do have a diastasis, use a splint—a sheet or a long scarf—when doing either sitting or back-lying abdominal exercises during your workout. Bring the sheet around your back and cross the two ends over your belly. Do not tie the ends in a knot, but grab the crossed-over ends and pull outward; you'll actually be bringing the two halves of the recti together. Splinting in this way doesn't hurt you or your baby and it gives a little external support to the separating recti muscles.

If you can't tell if you have a diastasis or not, opt for the splint. Bringing the recti together in this way really makes your transverse work more effective, and it is a good preventive measure. Bring the recti into the right position with the splint, and the muscle will start tightening up as you do the work.

I recommend using a splint, by the way, when you're in labor and ready to push. Pushing will be more effective if the recti are held together. So bring your sheet or scarf to the hospital or birthing center with you.

Now that you've done your fitness profile and you know a little more about your own personal strengths and weaknesses and what to do about them, we're ready to get started.

CHAPTER 7

The BAKS Basics:

Thirteen Easy Moves You Should Do Each Day, Even When You're Short on Time, Low on Energy, or Out of Motivation

Here we go. If you've read through the first six chapters you know a lot about breathing the right way, about muscles (the long and the short of them), and about the mechanics of your pregnant body and of childbirth. All of that constitutes the rationale for these exercises, which are designed primarily to strengthen and/or stretch the muscles that are being stressed as you carry around your ever-heavier uterus and that you'll be using during labor.

Now you're going to get your body working on what you've learned. These movements, the BAKS Basics, are the bread and butter of my Maternal Fitness program. Learn them. Practice them daily for at least seven days before you start the full exercise routine described in the next chapter. When we get to Chapter 8, where we discuss the Maternal Fitness workout, you'll see that the BAKS Basics are incorporated into the routine and combined with a lot of other stretches, squeezes, pulls, and lifts that all together are going to give you a great prenatal workout.

But I want you first to be very comfortable and on intimate terms with these muscle moves before you get more ambitious. And in fact, if you never take your exercise regimen to a higher level than the BAKS, you'll still be doing your body a great favor.

I call these movements the BAKS Basics because they include the following moves:

Breathing, **B**elly dancing
Abdominal work, **A**erobics
Kegels
Squatting, **S**tretching, **S**trengthening

Think Basics and you'll realize that you don't have to set aside a special time or place, always wear your exercise gear, or work exclusively on your exercises. Many of these movements you can practice anywhere whenever you have a few extra minutes—or even while you're doing other things. Work your transverse, for example, while you're sitting at your desk shuffling papers. Do your kegel squeezes while you're brushing your teeth, watching TV, or reading a book. Get in a little squatting time as you're talking to your mom on the phone or reading the newspaper.

If you do the BAKS Basics for seven days, you'll get that oxygen pumping through your bloodstream. You'll also start tightening up those all-important transverse and PC muscles, and you'll notice how much better your back feels and how much more aware and in control of your body you feel. In the pages that follow, I'll give you a little background first and then specific instructions for the exercises. At the end of this chapter you'll find an illustrated chart (pages 90–93) that you can refer to whenever you go through the BAKS routine. After you've become familiar with each exercise in the pages that follow, the chart will serve as an easy-to-use reference. You might want to photocopy the chart and keep it handy.

Breathing

This is not really an exercise at all but a way of life! If you breathe right, whether you're pregnant or not, everything inside you will work better, and you'll be able to do everything more efficiently.

And now, while you are pregnant, breathing the right way is more important than ever, because you're breathing for two. Your body's oxygen requirements have increased, since the oxygen you take in is circulating not only through you but also into the placenta to get to your baby. At the same time, you may have noticed that breathing is harder work than it used to be, because your uterus is pressing up against your diaphragm.

Correct breathing is *diaphragmatic breathing,* or expanding your belly as you take air into your lungs. Get into the habit of it and you will find yourself less short of breath and more relaxed. When you do the prenatal workout, you'll have more staying power because you'll be getting more oxygen. (And, as you know, by practicing proper breathing, you will be perfecting one of the critical skills used during the marathon of labor.)

I dislike the word "inhale," because it promotes a tendency to suck in the gut, and that's not what you want to do. You should do that when you exhale. When you get into the routine, you'll see that all the movements start and end with a belly breath and call for you to breathe through the stretches. I will not say "Take a deep breath," and I will certainly not say "Inhale." Usually I say "Expand," and that means fill your lungs by expanding your belly.

BAKS EXERCISE 1
Belly Breath

WHAT IT DOES. The belly breath improves circulation, promotes relaxation, prevents breathlessness, and gets the maximum amount of oxygen to you and your baby. It also gives you practice in the way to breathe during labor, and works the abdominal muscles correctly.

HOW TO DO IT

1. Sit in a chair or cross-legged on the floor with your back against the wall, and put your hands on your belly.
2. Pretend your lungs are in your belly. Expand your belly as you take air in through your nose and fill your lungs (see Figure 18).
3. Exhale through your mouth and empty your lungs as you bring your belly back toward your spine (see Figure 19).

DRILL. Spend at least ten minutes a day practicing relaxed belly breathing. Before going to bed is a good time.

TIPS. When you begin practicing belly breathing you may feel light-headed because you're not used to getting so much oxygen. Breathe in a more shallow way until the feeling passes, or cut down on the amount of time you spend doing belly breaths.

Figure 18 Belly
Breath:
(1) Take air in through
your nose as you
expand your belly.

Figure 19
(2) Exhale through your
mouth as you bring
your belly back to your
spine.

Avoid hyperventilating, or breathing too rapidly. Make sure that at the end of each belly breath you exhale completely, using your abdominal muscles.

Belly Dancing

I like to call these moves belly dancing, but they're really pelvic tilts. There are four belly dancing exercises in the BAKS Basics—three you'll learn now; the fourth you'll learn after we do some transverse abdominal work. Each of them, despite the exotic name, involves only a small, controlled movement to bring the bottom of the pelvis forward and then return it to the center.

Belly dancing deals with that S-curve in the lower back that we talked about earlier, the swaying-in caused when the uterus comes up out of the pelvic cavity and presses forward against the abdominal muscles. You'll remember that the recti (those muscles running up and down on either side of your belly button) are getting pushed out and are growing longer, and that's making your lower back muscles get shorter (see Figure 20). That means aches and pains! Pelvic tilts help reverse the process by shortening the recti from the bottom of the muscle and lengthening the lower back muscles, which keep getting shorter.

Besides doing them as a BAKS Basics exercise, use pelvic tilts as part of the mechanics of going from a sitting to a standing position, from a chair or from the floor.

BAKS EXERCISE 2
Belly Dancing I: Standing

WHAT IT DOES. Belly dancing while standing relieves stress on the lower back and prevents backaches by lengthening the lower back muscles and shortening the rectus abdominis from the bottom of the muscle.

HOW TO DO IT. Stand with your knees bent in a good, deep bend, legs apart at hip distance, one arm at your side and your other hand on your lower back with your fingers pointing toward the floor. If your fingers are not straight, bring your hips forward until your hand straightens.

Bring the bottom of your pelvis forward in a small movement, hold it to the count of 5, and return to the center, or to a flat back (see Figure 21). Think of a string tied to your tailbone. Pull the string downward as you move your pelvis forward.

DRILL. Do 10 tilts at a time at least once a day.

TIP. As you do the tilt, feel those muscles in your lower back lengthening—but don't arch your back or stick your buttocks out when you return to the starting position.

BAKS EXERCISE 3
Belly Dancing II: Hands Above Knees

WHAT IT DOES. This movement relieves stress on the lower back. It also prevents backaches by lengthening the lower back muscles and shortening the rectus abdominis from the bottom of the muscle.

Figure 20   MUSCLE CHANGES DURING PREGNANCY: When the uterus expands, the rectus abdominis gets longer and the lower back muscles get shorter.

Figure 21   BELLY DANCING I, STANDING: With your knees bent and your back flat, bring the bottom of your pelvis forward. Hold for 5 counts and then return to a flat back.

Figure 22 B ELLY D ANC-
ING II, H ANDS A BOVE
K NEES:
With your knees bent
and the weight of your
upper body forward,
your hands resting on
your knees, bring bot-
tom of pelvis forward.
Hold for 5 counts, and
return to flat back.

HOW TO DO IT. Stand with your knees bent, legs apart at hip distance, back flat. The weight of your hands, arms, and upper body should be resting on your thighs above your knees, with no pressure on your kneecaps.

Bring the bottom of your pelvis forward, hold to the count of 5, and return to center, or to a flat back (see Figure 22). Think of a string tied to your tailbone. Pull the string downward as you move your pelvis forward.

DRILL. Do 10 tilts at a time at least once a day.

TIP. Your knees should stay still! Don't move them as you tilt the bottom of your pelvis forward and back to center. Only the pelvis moves—think of your tailbone lengthening and going under. Keep your arms steady and don't curve your upper back.

BAKS EXERCISE 4
Belly Dancing III: On All Fours

WHAT IT DOES. This exercise relieves stress on the lower back and prevents backaches by lengthening the lower back muscles and shortening the rectus abdominis from the bottom of the muscle.

Figure 23 B ELLY D ANC-
ING III, ON A LL F OURS:
Get down on all fours,
with your knees bent
and hip distance apart,
your back flat, and your
toes on the floor. Bring
the bottom of your
pelvis forward, hold for
5 counts, and return to
a flat back. Don't curve
your upper back.

HOW TO DO IT. Get down on all fours, knees and hands flat on the floor, knees apart at hip distance, toes touching the floor.

Keeping your back flat and your upper back still, bring the bottom of your pelvis forward, hold to the count of 5, and return to the center, or to a flat back (see Figure 23). Don't forget to think of pulling on that string tied to your tailbone.

DRILL. Do 10 tilts at a time at least once a day.

TIPS. All-fours belly dancing should be done on an exercise mat or a rug to cushion your hands and knees. If you feel uncomfortable with your hands flat on the floor, rest on your fists instead.

As with all of the pelvic tilts, don't arch your lower back at any time during the exercise. Also, don't curve or move your upper back. Keep the movement small and controlled, and feel it in your lower back.

Abdominals

Here we return to my favorite muscle, the transverse. Locate it again by putting your hands, with your fingers spread apart, above and below your belly button and taking a belly-expanding breath. The muscle you feel moving out and then in, as you exhale, is your transverse.

Now imagine that transverse moving out and in, forward and backward, as if it were a sideways elevator. Think of your belly button as the engine that moves that elevator. Expand (take a belly breath). In this position your belly button is at the first floor. Exhale slowly, and begin to power your sideways elevator to its last stop—the fifth floor, which is located at your spine.

Of course, your navel isn't actually going to move all the way to your spine. I'm simply asking you to focus on the back-and-forth movement of your transverse muscle when you take a belly breath and do these exercises. Throughout the workouts I'll be referring to the different transverse positions as "floors." There's even a sixth floor, out through the back of your spine, and you'll travel there as your transverse gets stronger (see Figure 24).

In the two BAKS transverse abdominal exercises, you'll be moving your belly button back and forth between the floors and bringing that transverse *in,* strengthening it and developing power from the center. You already know from Anatomy 101 that all of the abdominal muscles are connected, so that whenever you work the transverse you're also working the recti—shortening it from the middle and closing up the separation. These exercises will make your back feel better, get your abdominal muscles back in shape faster after delivery, and, most important, get you prepared to use the Tupler Technique (breathing the right way, working a strengthened transverse

Figure 24 TRANSVERSE
ACTION:
The action of the trans-
verse muscle is for-
ward and backward.
Imagine this muscle as
a sideways elevator
that travels to six
floors. At first floor, the
belly button is in a
relaxed position; at fifth
floor, your belly button
is at the spine; at sixth
floor, your belly button
is going out through
the back of the spine.

muscle, and relaxing a strengthened PC muscle) to push your baby out. And I hope I've convinced you by now that if you haven't strengthened the transverse muscle and practiced using it beforehand, it will poop out on you during labor and you won't be able to push with it effectively.

Also remember that working the transverse will not harm your baby. Your uterus is very thick, and your baby is very well insulated in amniotic fluid inside the uterus.

When you do the BAKS abdominal exercises, nothing moves except your belly button, and you should feel this exercise in your back. If you don't feel a slight pulsing in your back as you move the muscle, you're not exercising it correctly. Go back and try again.

Do these exercises while you are sitting with your back supported so that it won't move and so that it will provide some resistance to the transverse. That's the position in which gravity will give you the most help. Later on, in the full routine in Chapter 8, you'll do the transverse exercises while lying on your back, which is harder. You need to do sitting transverse work *first,* so you will have the strength and the muscle awareness to hold the transverse in at fifth floor when you're lying on your back, where gravity makes it harder to do. Also, remember there's a good chance you'll be flat out when the big day comes. The sitting transverse exercises are the missing link in all abdominal work.

Start the abdominal exercises, and all of your exercises, with a belly breath, now that you know how to do it. Beginning with a belly breath gives you a running start on moving the muscle you want to move. It also puts the muscle in the proper starting position. When you take a belly breath, the transverse comes forward, so the only way it can go is *in* when you do the work part of the exercise, and that's where you want it, *in,* at fifth floor.

Remember to keep counting and to *count out loud.* If you're counting out loud, you're exhaling, and if you're exhaling, you're breathing, and "Keep breathing," as you know, is one of my favorite slogans. If you don't count, you're likely to hold your breath. When you're keeping that transverse muscle in, however, you obviously won't be able to take belly breaths—just small ones. If you find you're getting a little winded doing these transverse abdominal exercises, slow down—you're going too fast.

When you get comfortable with the belly breathing and the muscle moves (bringing it to fifth floor), use these techniques whenever your body does some work. Every time you sneeze (see Figures 25 and 26), every time you cough, every time you get up from a sitting to a standing position, first take a belly breath, so the muscle will be in the right starting position, and then bring the transverse *in*—back to fifth floor on the work part of the activity.

Having a bowel movement in the morning is a good time to practice your pushing technique (see Figures 27 and 28), so that by the time you get to labor, pushing will be second nature. The transverse muscle is always *in* on the work, not pushing out against your weakened recti and making that separation larger.

BAKS EXERCISE 5
Abdominals I: Elevators

WHAT IT DOES. This exercise strengthens the transverse abdominal muscles, which you will use in pushing during labor; it also shortens the recti from

Figure 25   BEFORE YOU SNEEZE:
Use your transverse muscle when you feel a sneeze or cough coming on. (1) Expand your belly *before* you sneeze or cough so the transverse muscle is in the right starting position to be "in" at fifth floor on the work.

Figure 26   AS YOU SNEEZE:
(2) Bring your belly to fifth floor as you sneeze or cough so as to shorten the rectus abdominis from the middle and prevent a diastasis from getting bigger.

Figure 27   PUSHING WITH THE TRANSVERSE MUSCLE:
(1) While having a bowel movement, sit on the toilet with your feet elevated so that you're in a squatting position. Start each push with a belly breath (expand the belly).

Figure 28 PUSHING:
(2) Bring the transverse to fifth floor and then out the back to sixth floor as you push (have bowel movement) and exhale (count to 5). Pelvic floor muscles are open and relaxed.

Figure 29
AB ELEVATOR:
(1) With one hand on your belly, one hand on your back, and your back supported, take a belly breath and bring the transverse to fifth floor. Hold it there as you count out loud to 30.

Figure 30
AB ELEVATOR:
(2) Still holding the transverse at fifth floor, bring the belly button "out the back" to sixth floor for 5 little pulses. Keep counting out loud. Do ten sets.

the middle while helping to close up the separation, and it prevents backaches during pregnancy.

HOW TO DO IT. Sit in a straight chair or on the floor with your back supported against the wall or the side of a couch, in a cross-legged position.

Place one hand on your belly, the other on the small of your back right above your waist.

Expand (take a belly breath). Exhale, and as you exhale slowly, bring your belly button from first floor back toward your spine (fifth floor), counting off the floors—2, 3, 4, 5. Hold at fifth floor and count out loud to 30 (see Figure 29). Don't forget to count. If you're counting out loud, you're exhaling, and if you're exhaling, I know you're breathing! It's easy to hold your breath while doing this exercise.

Staying at fifth floor, close your eyes and imagine your belly button going out the back of your spine and you are going to sixth floor for 5 counts—5 little pulses that flatten that belly button against the wall behind you. You should be able to feel this exercise with your hand on your back (see Figure 30).

Relax and end with a belly breath, bringing your belly button all the way back to the spine once more as you exhale.

DRILL. One set is hold-for-30, out-the-back-for 5. Do at least ten sets a day. As you get stronger do twenty sets, and then work up to fifty sets a day.

TIPS. Don't move your shoulders, back, or legs when doing elevators—all that moves is the belly button. When you first start doing the elevators, keep your back supported against the wall or chair. Remember to count out loud so that you continue to breathe. Do not be tempted to hold your breath when you hold any movements or do the pulses.

If you don't feel the muscles working in your back, you are not exercising as effectively as you could be.

The out-the back movement is an important movement and one you will need for pushing and for head lifts. The bigger your belly gets, the harder these movements will become.

BAKS EXERCISE 6
Abdominals II: Contracting

WHAT IT DOES. This exercise strengthens the transverse abdominal muscles, which you will use in pushing during labor. It also shortens the recti from the middle while helping to close the separation, and it prevents backaches during pregnancy.

HOW TO DO IT. Sit cross-legged with your back supported. Place one hand on your belly and the other hand on your back just above your waist.

Expand. Then exhale, and as you exhale bring your belly button back to third floor (halfway between first floor and fifth). This is your starting position. Now bring your belly button straight back to fifth floor. Release to third floor, and then squeeze back to fifth floor (each squeeze and release counts as one contraction). The emphasis, as in any exercise, is on holding the work part of the exercise. So hold the muscle briefly at fifth floor before releasing. Do *not* release to first floor. Remember you are counting, and exhaling, each time you go to fifth floor, which is the work part of the exercise. This forces you to breathe in on the release (third floor). Once again, counting out loud forces you to take little breaths after each contraction. No breath holding allowed (see Figure 31).

Relax and end with a belly breath, moving your belly all the way back to your spine once more as your exhale.

DRILL. Start with a set of 25 contractions 5 times a day. Within two or three days, you should be able to do a set of 100 contractions at a time, which should take about a minute and a half. Do five sets of these contractions a day.

When your transverse gets even stronger, make the movement smaller by squeezing and releasing between fourth and fifth floors (see Figure 32). Then progress to the smallest movement, fifth to sixth floor, with your belly button going out through the back of your spine, as in the elevator exercise (see Figure 33). Your goal before you deliver is to be doing ten sets of 100 at fifth to sixth floor per day.

Figure 31
AB CONTRACTING:
(1) Bring your belly button to third floor (halfway between first and fifth). Now pulse back to fifth floor, hold it there a moment as you count out loud. Put the emphasis on holding at fifth floor. One set is 100 third-to-fifth-floor pulses. Do five sets a day, two sets of 100 in the morning, two sets of 100 in the afternoon, and one set of 100 at bedtime.

Figure 32
(2) Make the exercise more strenuous by making the movement smaller (fourth to fifth floor).

Figure 33
(3) Make the exercise more vigorous by making the movement even smaller (fifth to sixth floor, as in the elevator exercise).

Do 300 in the morning, 300 in the afternoon and 400 at bedtime.

TIPS. Because a diastasis (separation) gives less support to the abdomen—if the ridge between the two parts of the rectus abdominus is three fingers wide or more—give your transverse some help by bringing the two halves of the recti together by wrapping a sheet or scarf around your belly, holding the ends securely with both hands as you do the transverse exercises (see Figure 34).

Be diligent in doing your third to fifth, then fourth to fifth, then fifth to sixth floor transverse exercises. If you strengthen the muscles while you're in a sitting position, you'll be able to do back-lying exercises better. Remember, if you get out of breath when doing these exercises, you are going too fast. Slow down. The bigger your belly gets, the harder these exercises will become, but don't give up. These exercises are the most important ones for strengthening your abdominals for pushing, preventing backaches, and getting your abdominals back in shape faster! I urge you to do contracting when you're in your car, at your desk at work, or watching TV. Keep doing them throughout the day.

When you've worked on strengthening your transverse for a few days, you'll be ready to do Belly Dancing IV, a pelvic tilt done while lying on your back. It's essentially the beginning move of a head lift. If you have done other workouts in the past, you were probably told to start head lifts or sit-ups by pressing your back to the floor. When you press your back to the floor, however, you have a tendency to push your transverse forward. What is different in, and critical to, our exercise is that you will be holding your transverse securely at fifth floor as you press your back to the floor.

Figure 34 USING A
SPLINT:
While doing sitting
transverse abdominal
exercises, bring the
two halves of the rec-
tus abdominis together
by wrapping a sheet or
a long scarf around
your abdomen and
holding it there while
you do the exercises.

Figure 35 SITTING UP
FROM A BACK-LYING
POSITION:
(1) Roll to one side
without lifting your
head.

Figure 36
(2) Hold the transverse
muscle at fifth floor
and raise yourself up to
a sitting position with
your arms.

Figure 37
(3) Get onto all fours.

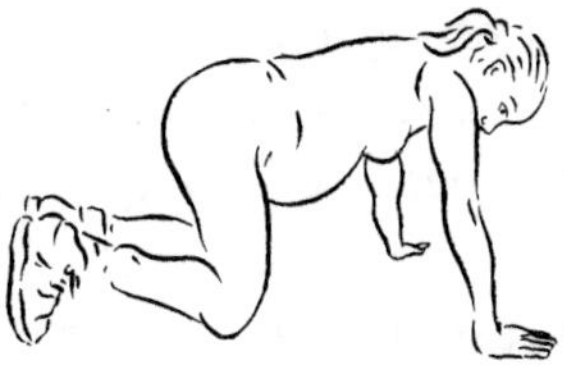

Figure 38
(4) From the on-all-
fours position bring
one leg up, placing
your hand above that
knee.

Figure 39
(5) Now bring your
other leg up with your
other hand above that
knee into the hands-
above-knees position.

This is the first time you'll do an exercise while you're lying down. Remember, if you feel light-headed or dizzy, roll over onto your side. This also means you're going to have to get up. As I mentioned in Chapter 5 it's important to get up and down correctly so as not to make the separation in your recti bigger or put stress on your back. So let's review this, because it's very important. Here's how you get up out of a supine position:

- Bend your knees and then roll to one side. Do not lift your head (see Figure 35).
- Bear all of your weight on your arm muscles, hold the transverse in at fifth floor, and push yourself to a sitting position (see Figure 36).
- Get onto all fours (see Figure 37). If you want, stay there for a minute and get in a few pelvic tilts.
- Get into the hands-above-knees position by bringing your right leg up and placing your right hand above your right knee (see Figure 38).
- Now bring your left leg up and place your left hand above your left knee (see Figure 39). Stay here for a moment and do a few pelvic tilts.
- Hold your transverse at fifth floor and roll up, rounding your back, from the base of your spine one vertebra at a time.

BAKS EXERCISE 7
Belly Dancing IV: Back-Lying

WHAT IT DOES. This exercise relieves stress on the lower back and prevents backaches by lengthening the lower back muscles and shortening the rectus abdominis from the bottom and from the middle of the muscle. Actually, it shortens the recti from the middle only if you work your transverse muscle correctly. This will also make the separation smaller.

HOW TO DO IT. Get into a supine position from a sitting position by using your arms to lower yourself onto your side (see Figure 36). Remember to hold your transverse in at fifth floor as you do this. Then roll onto your back, being careful to keep your head on the floor.

With your back on the mat, make sure your feet are on the floor, knees are bent and at hip distance apart, one hand is on your belly, and one hand is on the small of your back.

Expand your belly by taking a belly breath (see Figure 40).

Bring the transverse muscle to fifth floor (see Figure 41).

Hold it there as you bring your pubic bone toward your navel and count, or exhale (see Figure 42).

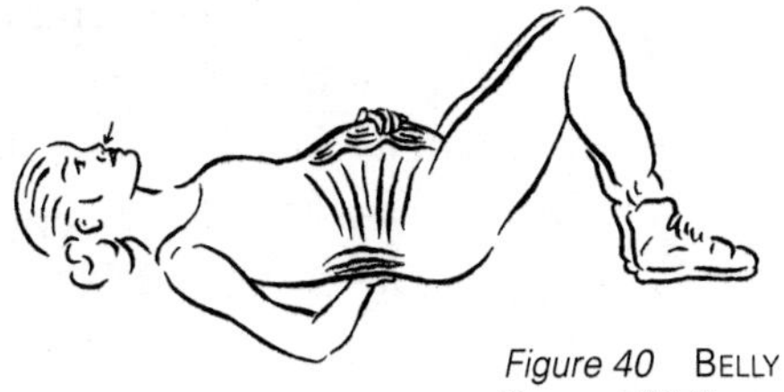

DRILL. Do 10 tilts at a time at least once a day, beginning each tilt with a belly breath.

TIPS. If you feel light-headed or dizzy at any time, roll onto your side and discontinue the exercise.

Remember to keep your buttocks on the floor. Think of your abdominals moving your pelvis.

The most important part of this exercise is holding the transverse in as you press your back to the floor. Pushing the transverse forward when you press your back on the floor is a bad habit that's hard to break. So really concentrate. Close your eyes and feel with your hand whether the transverse stays in or pops out when you press your back to the floor. It's important for you to know if the transverse is in or out. You cannot do the head lifts in the Maternal Fitness routine until you've done this exercise correctly.

Aerobics

An aerobic exercise is any sustained activity that conditions the heart and lungs by increasing the efficiency of oxygen intake by the body. Swimming, running, and walking are aerobic activities. Although it is not a "move," like belly dancing, I'm including an aerobic exercise here because "aerobic" is part of

Figure 40 BELLY DANCING IV: BACK-LYING: (1) With knees bent, one hand on your belly, and one hand slightly under small of your back, expand your belly.

Figure 41
(2) Bring the transverse to fifth floor.

Figure 42
(3) Hold transverse at fifth floor as you bring your pubic bone toward your navel.

the *A* in BAKS Basics, and I want you to remember the importance of getting regular aerobic exercise. To prepare for your marathon of labor you need cardiovascular strength as well as strong muscles. Our Maternal Fitness routine will not give you an aerobic workout, but I support your efforts to increase your heart-lung fitness.

Here are some points to remember when you do aerobics:

1. If the aerobic exercise or sport of your choice involves balance or puts you at risk of falling, switch to another form of aerobic work. Remember that during pregnancy your center of gravity is higher and farther forward than normal, and joint laxity from the hormone relaxin can make you clumsier and more unstable on your feet. You may be at greater than normal risk of falling during step classes, high-tech aerobic classes with complicated routines, tennis, and running. If you fall, take care not to fall on your belly. Fall on your side or buttocks. A sharp blow to the placenta, which is attached to your uterine wall, could cause it to detach.

2. Be careful not to get overheated. Your body temperature is already elevated because you're pregnant. When you do aerobic exercise your body temperature goes up even higher. Your body compensates by perspiring, but the baby has no way of cooling down. So stay cool by drinking lots of water, wearing light and comfortable clothing, and exercising in a cool environment. Also avoid hot tubs and saunas. Swimming is great, as it's hard to get overheated when you're in cool water.

3. Losing fluids and becoming dehydrated is also a problem during aerobic exercise, as you can lose amniotic fluids, which will cause premature labor. So drink lots of water when you're doing any form of aerobics.

4. Certain aerobic exercises are better than others because of the postural changes of pregnancy. Your hip flexors are getting shorter, which can cause backaches, so this might be a good time to avoid working out on the stationary bike or a stair machine, as these exercises also have a shortening effect. If you do want to keep using your stationary bike or stair machine, be sure you do hip flexor stretches before and after exercising (see Figure 69 on page 103). Walking, swimming, and using the treadmill may be more comfortable for you now, because these are extension or muscle-lengthening activities.

5. Tennis is especially hard on abdominals because the crossover movements of the upper body make the separation of the recti larger (see Figure 15 on page 52). It is hard on the knee and ankle joints because of the side-to-side movements involved.

6. ACOG's original guidelines stated that during aerobic activity the heartbeat should not go higher than 140 beats a minute. However, the guidelines have now been revised: If you are in your late thirties or your forties and you've never exercised,

140 beats a minute is too high. So instead of taking your pulse, remember the concept of *perceived exertion*. You should be able to carry on a conversation while you are exercising. If you are huffing and puffing, you're doing too much and your heart rate is too high. If your body tells you to slow down, do it!

7. ACOG also advises that the strenuous portion of your exercise routine should not exceed fifteen to twenty minutes. Lower-intensity aerobic activities may be conducted for as long as forty-five minutes.

Again, listen to your body! If something doesn't feel right, don't do it.

Kegels

You've already learned everything you ever wanted to know about your pubococcygeus, or PC, the main muscle of the pelvic floor—namely, that it supports everything in your pelvic area (that bag of groceries), that it aids in elimination and enhances sexual appreciation, and that your pregnant uterus is wreaking havoc on the poor thing, making it longer and weaker. And you know that you have two goals for this PC muscle: (1) to make it shorter and stronger, because a strong muscle stretches better, and this is one muscle you want to be stretchable: and (2) to practice relaxing it, the better to open it up (think of it as a flower) when it's time for your baby to be born.

When you get into the Maternal Fitness routine, you'll be isolating and separating what you're doing with the abdominal muscles from your work with the pelvic muscles. I'll say, "Relax your abdominals, hold that PC muscle in, and give me a kegel for the count of 10"—because when you're in labor, you'll want to work those muscles separately, so that one's tight and the other is open.

A lot of pregnancy books will tell you to do your kegels while you're urinating. Wrong, wrong, wrong! It's okay to locate (feel) the muscle by *pretending* to stop your flow of urine, but never do PC-hold exercises *while* you're urinating, because that might promote a urinary tract infection—something pregnant women are more than usually prone to.

As with the transverse, gravity plays a part in the effectiveness with which you can exercise the pelvic floor muscles. This makes sense. When you're standing, all of your groceries press down on the PC muscles. When you're sitting, less weight bears down on the muscle. Try putting your legs up against the wall; that's an even better gravity-assisted position, because your groceries are going in the other direction. (Doing PC exercises in a squatting position is like weight lifting: you have to hold those muscles in or everything will start hanging down! That's why women who live in countries where squatting is common practice have strong pelvic floor muscles.)

You'll do the two BAKS kegel exercises initially while you're sitting down with your legs apart and your abdominals relaxed. But as you develop muscle strength you will find it easier and easier to do kegels while you're standing or squatting. And it's great to get in as many PC holds as you can in the course of a day. Do a set of kegels while you're standing at the sink, chopping vegetables, waiting for a bus, or driving your car. Relax those muscles. While you're relaxing, you can do a set of transverse abdominal exercises. If on your fitness evaluation you couldn't hold your PC in for a count of 10, it will take you a while to strengthen it, so keep doing your kegels while you're sitting down, or with your legs up if that works better.

I want you to sit with your legs apart; if you sit cross-legged or with your legs close together you will tend to use the muscles in your buttocks, and that does nothing much to help your PC muscle. I also want your abdominals relaxed because these two sets of muscles work in reverse—tighten down below, keep loose on top. When you're ready to push that baby out, it'll be tight on top, open below. As with the transverse abdominal exercises, in one of the exercises (Kegel II: Elevators) you're going to imagine the muscle as an elevator, but this time it will go up and down, not sideways.

BAKS EXERCISE 8
Kegels I: The Ten-Second Hold

WHAT IT DOES. The ten-second kegel strengthens the pelvic floor muscles, helps prevent urine leaks, enhances sexual pleasure, and prepares the pelvic floor muscles to open and relax during delivery.

HOW TO DO IT. Sit comfortably with your legs apart and your back supported against a wall or a chair, and relax your abdominals. Now pretend you have to urinate but you're going to stop the flow. Hold in the PC muscles as tight as you can as you count to ten. Then relax the muscle, feel it open like a flower, and hold it in again.

DRILL. Do 20 of these ten-second holds at a time 5 times a day. That's at least 100 PC holds daily.

TIPS. If you have difficulty holding your PC in for ten seconds at a time, start with a five-second hold, or do the kegel exercise in a gravity-assisted position with your legs up on the wall (see Figure 45 on page 87), as you will do in later stretching exercises.

Remember, the relaxation part of this exercise is important. You need to be able to release and relax this muscle as a preparation for pushing during labor.

As I mentioned earlier, a good time to practice this relaxation is while having your bowel movement in the morning. The transverse is pushed back; the pelvic floor is open and relaxed.

BAKS EXERCISE 9
Kegels II: Elevators

WHAT IT DOES. This exercise strengthens the pelvic floor muscles, helps prevent urine leaks, enhances sexual pleasure, and prepares the pelvic floor muscles to open and relax during delivery.

HOW TO DO IT. Sit comfortably with your legs apart and your back supported, and relax your abdominal muscles. Imagine a penny at the entrance to your vagina. Now pick up the penny with the lips of your vagina.

Think of an elevator that goes to five floors, the belly button being the fifth floor. Bring the penny up from the first floor and take it through the second, third, and fourth floors to the fifth floor. Hold the penny at fifth floor and count to 5.

Slowly bring the penny back down through the fourth, third, and second floors to first floor. Now imagine your vagina opening up like a flower, and let the penny go. Then hold the muscle in again.

DRILL. Do 10 elevators at a time at least 5 times a day.

TIPS. If the downward movement is difficult for you and if, as you're coming down, your elevator crashes to the basement, don't worry. As the muscle gets stronger, the downs will be more controlled.

This exercise, like the kegel I exercise, is also a ten-second hold. Up for five seconds and then holding for five seconds. It's just a different way of working this muscle.

Squatting

I consider squatting the ideal position from which to give birth because the outlet of your pelvis is opened up 27 percent in diameter, your weight is supported on your thighs, and gravity is on your side. Practice squatting as part of your BAKS Basics and you'll be better prepared to use this position, if you choose, during labor.

Squatting is a wonderful exercise in general, one that can greatly benefit many parts of your body. It's a natural position, in fact, although most of us rarely use it. Preschool children squat easily and all the time. Later they begin to sit in chairs for prolonged periods. As a result, their calf muscles tighten, the joints of their ankles and backs become stiff, and they grow up to be people who don't squat. We all need to re-experience the pleasure of squatting!

Squatting strengthens muscles in the knees, thighs, and buttocks. It also strengthens the abdominal muscles, especially the obliques, because it realigns the pelvic geometry so that the abdominals are more efficiently brought into use as you go about your daily routines. And it helps to stretch and relax your lower back by reducing that S-curve in the lower region, relieving the muscles and ligaments that support your spine and lessening pressure on the disks between the spinal bones.

Squatting also stimulates circulation to the pelvic area and strengthens and stretches the pelvic floor muscles, and you know that's something to be desired when you're ready to give birth. And more: during elimination, the squatting position supports and aligns the bowel to produce an easier and more complete evacuation. The man who invented the toilet was a plumber, not an anatomist; he did not recognize the natural advantage that squatting offers the body.

Reinventing the toilet is not a practical solution, but you can approximate the squatting posture—and help unkink your bowel—by using a small footstool (about 8 inches high) to elevate your feet when you're having a bowel movement. Or, if you have a small square wastebasket in your bathroom, just turn it on its side and put your feet on it. The bowel is supported and elimination is aided. And if constipation has been a problem during your pregnancy, you'll need all the help you can get!

Squatting is not hard on normal knees—not if you get down and stay down for a while, avoid bouncing, and bear your weight on the outsides of your feet. It's getting *up* from the squat that's hard on the knees. If you normally have problem knees, or if you have pain in your pubic area or have varicose veins, consult your doctor before doing these exercises.

Especially when you're first starting out, hold on to something; this position is known as a *supported squat*. You might hold on to the end of an immovable piece of furniture, a railing, or a doorjamb and ease yourself down into a squat. During labor, two people can support you under your arms in a supported squat. If you've practiced squatting during your pregnancy it will be a more natural position for you during labor. And after the baby is born, remember to hold your transverse in and keep squatting whenever you pick something up.

BAKS EXERCISE 10
Squatting

WHAT IT DOES. Squatting strengthens the oblique abdominal muscles, the knees, and the pelvic floor muscles. It also stretches the lower back, calves, and pelvic floor muscles.

HOW TO DO IT. Stand with your feet flat and wide apart. Hold on to an immovable object like a railing or doorjamb, and descend gradually and without bouncing into a squat, bending your knees and making sure your heels are on the floor. Shift your weight to the outsides of your feet; keep your arms straight and at shoulder height, and keep your head up (see Figure 43). Hold the squat for fifteen to twenty seconds.

DRILL. Start by doing a fifteen- or twenty-second supported squat several times a day. Work up to holding the position for a full minute at a time. Then gradually work your way up to five minutes at a time 5 times a day.

Figure 43
SUPPORTED SQUAT:
Hold on to an immovable object with your arms straight at shoulder height, your heels on the floor, and your weight on the outsides of your feet. Hold for 15 to 20 seconds. Work up to 5 minutes 5 times a day.

TIPS. If you have trouble keeping your heels on the floor, try straightening your arms and pulling farther away from the object you are holding on to. If that doesn't work, try putting a rolled-up blanket under your heels, wearing low heels, or sitting on a short stack of books.

You may find your legs go to sleep at first, but your circulation will improve as you continue practicing your squats. Try reading a book or magazine while squatting. That makes the time go faster. As your belly get bigger, continue to widen your squatting stance to accommodate it.

Get out of the squat correctly. *Do not stand up from this position.* This is very hard on your knees. Get out of the squat by lowering yourself to a sitting position one hand at a time. Before getting to a standing position, get onto all fours (see Figure 23, page 68) and then into the hands-above-knees position (see Figure 22 on page 68).

Stretching

If you have a cat, watch it lean into a good stretch. Its back arches way up, then way down so that its belly is almost dragging on the floor. Its front legs and chest go way out; then the back legs and butt go way out. Finally a look of utter contentment crosses the cat's face. Cats stretch better than anybody, and don't they just *look* like the most relaxed creatures on earth?

Stretching, as you already know, is nature's prescription for relaxing the body. It's stress-relieving and it keeps you flexible where you want to be flexible. And you know that stretching is also the way to lengthen those muscles that have been shortening up in your pregnant body. You've done some of that work already with the belly dancing, or pelvic tilts, and with the squatting that gently stretches out the muscles in your lower back. Now we're going to add three exercises that will stretch the muscles in your chest (those pectorals that have been getting shorter as your shoulders and neck have come forward) and in your inner thighs and the backs of your legs.

People do stretching exercises in two basic ways. One is incorrect and the other is correct. Here's the incorrect way: Stretch the muscle you're working as far as it can go and then perform quick, repetitive, bouncing movements. This is called ballistic stretching, and it's very harmful for the body. Because of a protective-reflex contraction, it can actually, in fact, shorten the muscle you want to lengthen, and it increases your chances of tearing muscle fibers. Never bounce! Never stretch beyond the point at which you feel discomfort!

Static stretching is the right way to go, and that involves a slow, deliberate stretch through the muscle's full range of movement until you feel a tightness or resistance in the muscle. *Stop before you feel pain.* Hold the stretch for up to thirty seconds and then relax.

I love the idea, as you know, of putting your mind in your muscle. Develop the habit of mentally focusing on the muscle you're working. This way, you'll do the exercises more efficiently, and you'll be practicing a technique you'll need to use on the big day to help deal with the stretching sensations of those muscles in your pelvic floor area. As you do these stretches, close your eyes and visualize the muscle. First, take a moment or two to "see" the muscle relaxed (tense muscles are in a shortened position), then "see" it lengthening as you breathe through the stretch.

BAKS EXERCISE 11
Stretching I: Chest Muscles (Pectorals)

WHAT IT DOES. This stretching exercise lengthens the chest muscles, or pectorals, and shortens the upper back muscles.

HOW TO DO IT. Sit in a chair or on the floor with your back nice and flat. Hold on to the ends of a long sock, a small towel, or anything that's not elastic, and bring the towel behind your head. Keep your elbows below your shoulders. Gently bring your elbows back behind your shoulders without arching your back (see Figure 44). Hold the stretch for thirty seconds. Relax.

DRILL. Do at least 10 chest stretches a day.

Figure 44 STRETCHING THE CHEST MUSCLES: Sit with your back supported. Hold the ends of a small towel behind your head and bring your elbows back behind your shoulders. Hold for 30 seconds.

TIPS. You'll probably feel some tension in your upper arm muscles. Keep your arms relaxed and focus on lengthening those chest muscles. Don't bend your wrists or arch your back.

If you spend a lot of time sitting at a desk, try to do a pectoral stretch at least once every hour.

BAKS EXERCISE 12
Stretching II: Inner Thighs

WHAT IT DOES. This stretch lengthens the inner thigh, or adductor, muscles.

HOW TO DO IT. Using your arms, and from a sitting position on the floor, lower your-self to your side. Roll onto your back with your buttocks against a wall. Keeping your head on the floor and your buttocks against the wall, slowly put your legs up on the wall. Slowly separate your legs until you feel a stretch along your inner thighs. Hold the stretch for 30 seconds (see Figure 45). Then relax. While you're relaxing, do some kegels, remembering to relax the abdominals first.

Bring your legs together, bend your knees, roll to the side, and hold the transverse in as you push yourself to a sitting position with your arms.

DRILL. Do at least one thirty-second stretch each day. Work up to three thirty-second stretches twice a day.

TIPS. Put a pillow under your head if you want. Remember, if you feel light-headed or dizzy, roll to your side and rest for a moment or discontinue the exercise.

If you are very flexible and your legs flop over when you get them up against the wall, this isn't a good exercise for you. Skip it. To prevent injury to your joints, it's important not to overstretch.

It's a good idea to do these inner thigh stretches in the morning. However, by doing these stretches again in the evening, after you've been on your feet all day, you can help reduce swelling in your legs.

BAKS EXERCISE 13
Stretching III: Backs of Legs

WHAT IT DOES. This exercise lengthens the muscles running along the backs of the legs.

HOW TO DO IT. Sit on the floor with one leg straight out in front of you, foot lined up with the thigh, and with your other leg bent at the knee, foot resting against your other knee. Rest your hands below the knee of your straight leg (see Figure 46). Close your eyes, relax your straightened knee, and see the muscles running down the back of your leg relax.

Now breathe through the stretch. Expand your belly and bring your transverse to the spine as you exhale and slide your hands forward toward your extended foot as far as you can go. See the muscles running down the back of the leg lengthening (see Figure 47). Hold the stretch for ten to twenty seconds. Hold the transverse at fifth floor as you roll up straight, from the base of your spine one vertebra at a time. Repeat with the other leg.

DRILL. Do at least one ten- to twenty-second stretch once a day. This is also a good stretch to do after aerobic exercise.

TIPS. Remember that the transverse is in on the work of the stretch and in as you straighten your body back to a sitting position.

Keep your foot in a relaxed, or flexed, position. Don't point your toes.

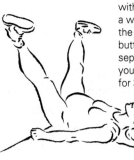

Figure 45 STRETCHING THE INNER THIGHS:
From a side-lying position with your buttocks against a wall, put your legs up on the wall. Still keeping your buttocks against the wall, separate your legs until you feel the stretch. Hold for 30 seconds.

Figure 46 STRETCHING THE BACKS OF YOUR LEGS:
(1) Sit on the floor with one leg straight, foot lined up with thigh, and one leg bent, the foot resting against the opposite knee. Place your hands below the straight knee. Relax that knee and the back of that leg. Now expand your belly.

Figure 47
(2) Bring the transverse to fifth floor as you exhale and move your hands toward your extended foot. Hold for 10 to 20 seconds. Keeping the transverse at fifth floor, roll up from the base of your spine one vertebra at a time.

Muscle Strengthening

Now that you have become familiar with the stretching movements in the BAKS Basics, I want to be sure you understand the connection between *stretching* muscles and *strengthening* them.

You want to strengthen the muscles that are getting longer and weaker because of the postural changes and joint laxity that come with pregnancy and because of your expanding uterus.

In particular, you want to strengthen your abdominals and the muscles of your upper back and pelvic floor. A strong muscle can lift, carry, hold, push, pull, and do whatever work is required of it. Throughout the BAKS Basics and later, in the Maternal Fitness routine, you are working to contract and shorten those muscles you need to be strong—the muscles you need to do the work of carrying, lifting, and pushing.

At the same time, your muscles must be flexible—that is, stretchy. Muscles that are too tight cannot move your limbs in a coordinated and controlled manner, which is especially important as your body goes through the changes associated with pregnancy. A muscle that is both strong and flexible is a *toned* muscle, capable of doing work, pulling your bones together, and enabling your body to move efficiently and smoothly.

This balance between strengthening and stretching the muscles is central to the Maternal Fitness routine. Follow the steps as I have outlined them, and you will not be in danger of stressing ligaments, grinding joints, or fraying tendons. You will be developing toned muscles that will serve you well right up to and through your marathon of labor.

While exercising during pregnancy, you know that it is especially important to prevent a diastasis—the separation of the recti muscles—from getting larger. This routine focuses on maintaining the strength of the abdominals while you do upper and lower body work. So I'll be asking you to hold your transverse muscle back at the fifth floor on the work part of all the exercises. If you find you cannot hold the transverse at fifth floor when you are doing any exercise, do not proceed with that activity.

Those are the BAKS Basics. Make them a part of your life and practice them for at least seven days before you work up to the full routine outlined in Chapter 8. After just seven days your transverse will be tightened up and on its way to becoming a powerful pushing machine. You'll have belly breathing down pat, and you'll be ready to breathe correctly through the workout. Your lower back will be feeling better. In general, you'll be in better touch with and in control of you body.

You don't have to go through the entire BAKS routine in one fell swoop. In fact, I've been suggesting that you take random opportunities throughout your day to get in some kegels or some transverse contracting or elevators. But you can do the whole routine at once if you want to. One BAKS session should take fifteen to twenty minutes. You can follow the sequence as I've presented it here or vary the pattern, if another sequence seems to flow better. As I said in Chapter 5, it's important to do the BAKS Basics regularly—even after you begin the Maternal Fitness routine, which you should do three times a week. On the days that you don't do the Maternal Fitness workout, do the BAKS moves, either as a routine or by incorporating the moves into your daily activities.

Now I'm going to get you going on the full prenatal Maternal Fitness workout I put my clients through when they come for one-on-one sessions. As you do the routine you'll be incorporating all of the movements you've learned here.

BAKS Basics

BELLY BREATHING:
Sit in a comfortable position. Place hands on belly. Take air in
through nose and expand belly. Exhale through mouth and bring
belly back to spine. Do 10 minutes a day; bedtime is a good time.
Tips: Exhale completely at the end of each breath.

BELLY DANCING (PELVIC TILTS)

STANDING:
Stand with knees bent and
one hand on back so it is flat.
Bring bottom of pelvis forward, hold 5 seconds; return
to flat back. Do 10 a day.

HANDS ABOVE KNEES:
Weight of hands, arms, and
upper body is resting on
thighs above knees. Start with
knees bent and flat back.
Without moving knees, bring
bottom of pelvis forward, hold
5 seconds, return to flat back.
Do 10 a day.

ON ALL FOURS:
On all fours, position yourself with flat back and knees at hip distance apart. Without moving upper back, bring your pubic bone toward your navel and count or exhale.

BACK-LYING (FOUNDATION OF HEAD LIFT):
Do after learning transverse exercises. Assume a back-lying position with knees bent, one hand on belly and one hand on back. Expand belly, exhale as you bring the transverse to the spine, hold it there as you bring your pubic bone toward your navel and count or exhale.

ABDOMINALS
TRANSVERSE:
Back must be supported and not move during exercises. Use belly button as "engine" to move transverse muscle, one hand on belly and one hand on back.

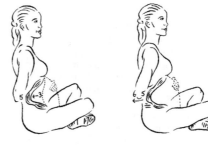

TUPLER TECHNIQUE ELEVATOR:
Belly to fifth floor. Hold at fifth while you count to 30. Now press it back fifth to sixth floor as you count to 5. Counting will force you to breathe. Do 10 a day.

CONTRACTING:
Belly goes from third to fifth floor. Hold for a moment at fifth floor. One set is 100; do 5 sets a day. Progress to fourth to fifth floor and then fifth to sixth as in elevator.

PRACTICE PUSHING
WITH ABDOMINALS:
Practice while having a bowel
movement. Feet are elevated.
Expand belly, transverse to
fifth and then to sixth floor as
you exhale and count to 10 as
you are having a bowel movement. Pelvic floor is open and
relaxed. This is exhale pushing. Please, no breath holding!

AEROBICS:
Be able to carry on a conversation while doing any exercise or activity (perceived
exertion). Drink water before,
during, and after exercise.
Don't get overheated. Do
"safe" exercises that won't
put you at risk for falling. No
more than 45 minutes of aerobic exercise at a moderate
intensity. Listen to your body.

KEGELS:
Do kegels in a sitting position
with legs apart and abdominals relaxed (harder standing
and squatting; easier with
legs up on wall). Holds: (10
seconds) Do 20 holds 5 times
a day. Elevators: Up 5 counts,
hold 5 counts and slowly
down and open like a flower,
then squeeze. Do 10 a day.
Muscle getting stronger when
down part of exercise
becomes more controlled.

SQUATTING:
Hold on to an immovable
object and get into a squatting
position. Arms are straight at
shoulder height; weight is
shifted to outsides of feet;
heels are on floor. To get out
of squat, use one hand at a
time to bring you to a sitting
position. Hold 1 to 5 minutes
a day.

STRETCHING:
Before stretching, relax muscle first, allowing it to lengthen. Breathe through the stretch, seeing the muscles lengthen. Expand belly, transverse to spine as you exhale and stretch.

CHEST (pectorals): In a seated position, hold towel behind head, bring elbows back behind shoulders, and hold for 30 counts. Don't arch back.

BACK OF LEG (hamstring): Hands below knee. Breathe through stretch as you bring hands toward foot.

INNER THIGH (adductor): From a side-lying position with buttocks on wall, put legs up on wall, keeping buttocks against wall. Put pillow under head; 30-second stretches in morning and evening.

STRENGTHENING:
All exercises must be done with transverse muscle "IN" (fifth floor) on the work part of an exercise or activity to protect a "weakened" rectus abdominis. If you can't hold the transverse at fifth floor while doing any exercise or activity, it is an indication not to proceed with the activity.

CHAPTER 8

The Maternal Fitness Workout

Picture this: I've come to your home for your one-on-one Maternal Fitness workout. You're wearing your comfy duds, there's a mat on the floor, and your favorite music is playing. We do a little warming up, and then we proceed through a series of exercises that move all those muscles that need shortening or lengthening. And I keep talking the whole time, taking you through the routine.

That's how I want this chapter to work and to feel like—as if you have your own personal fitness trainer right there in your living room, leading you through the routine. In the course of working with hundreds of clients, I've designed and refined the Maternal Fitness routine to be a fluid process that moves naturally through the standing, on-hands-and-knees, sitting, and side-lying positions. This routine provides a complete body workout and takes sixty to ninety minutes, depending on how many repetitions and sets you do of the different exercises. We recommend that you do the routine at least three times a week. You will have your high-energy days and your low-energy days. On your high-energy days you can do your aerobic workout and also our routine. You can also alternate, doing your aerobic workout on the days when you don't do this workout. If you're a regular exerciser, you'll quickly see how you can incorporate parts of this routine into your other workouts and sports. Remember to do the BAKS moves on days when you don't do the Maternal Fitness workout.

Before I talk you through the Maternal Fitness routine, I have two suggestions on how to use this material: (1) if your partner is keeping you company as you exercise, have him or her put you through your paces and read out what you're supposed to be doing; or (2) record the workout on a tape cassette, and play the tape whenever you're ready to exercise (go through the routine a couple of times first before you record it, so you'll know how much time to allow for each of the moves).

All of the exercises are illustrated; you'll probably have to check out the pictures the first couple of times you do these moves. In order to simplify the workouts, *the illustrations have been drawn as mirror images of what you are supposed to be doing.* In other words, when I tell you to raise your right arm, you'll see a mirror image of that movement in the illustration, though technically the figure is raising her left arm. Look at the drawings as if you were looking into a mirror, and follow the text.

At the end of this chapter you'll find an illustrated chart that will lead you through the entire routine. Once you are completely familiar with the workout, you may find that just listening to your tape is enough. I recommend you photocopy the chart and post it on a wall near your workout area.

Along the way I'll be telling you how to check that the parts of your body are lined up in the right position. I'll also be saying, "Let's get in a few kegels right here before we move on," or "Give me some pelvic tilts while you're down there on your hands and knees." This is how you're going to incorporate all those good BAKS Basics exercises you've been working on.

And of course I'll keep reminding you to exercise that transverse, bringing it back to the spine (or to fifth floor) as you do the work of the movement. Sometimes I say, "Bring the belly button to the spine," or "to fifth floor"—same thing. The belly button is right in the middle of the transverse and makes a good focal point to help move this muscle. Remember, all that moves is the belly button. No shoulders, no back, no leg movements. So when you're stretching out your upper back or doing leg lifts, you're always strengthening the transverse and getting it ready for your marathon. You can hold your transverse at fifth floor and still breathe, though it takes some practice because you're not used to doing this. Initially it feels as if you're holding your breath, but the exercise becomes easier the stronger your transverse muscle gets.

Lay out your exercise mat, get out your Dyna-Band and light weights, put on some fun music, and let's get started!

Standing Warm-Up

Let's begin by warming up.

We'll do some *arm stretches* first (see Figure 48). Stand with your feet apart at hip distance and your knees bent. Remember not to stick those buttocks out. Keep your knees above your toes and your back nice and flat.

Let's take a belly breath and expand your belly as you stretch both arms over your head. Exhale through your mouth as you bring your arms down and your belly button to your spine. Once again. Let's do 2 of these stretches. Expand, taking air in through your nose as you raise your arms over your head. Now exhale through your mouth as you lower your arms and bring your belly button back to your spine.

Now we're going to stretch out your *upper back* (see Figure 49). Keeping your knees bent, bring your arms forward and hold on to the doorknob of a door that's tightly closed or hold some other immovable object. Curve your back, and as you pull away from the doorknob, feel that stretch in your upper back. Continue to breathe normally.

Now let's stretch out your *lower back* (see Figure 50). Put your hands right above your knees in the hands-above-knees position you learned in the BAKS Basics. Remember to keep your knees bent and your back as flat as possible. Now expand your belly, and bring that transverse to your spine as you do a pelvic tilt. Feel those lower back muscles lengthening. Imagine a string tied to your tailbone, pulling it down as you tilt. This is a small movement. There should be no movement in your knees. Let's do 5 of these. This should feel great in your lower back. Now hold that transverse at fifth floor as

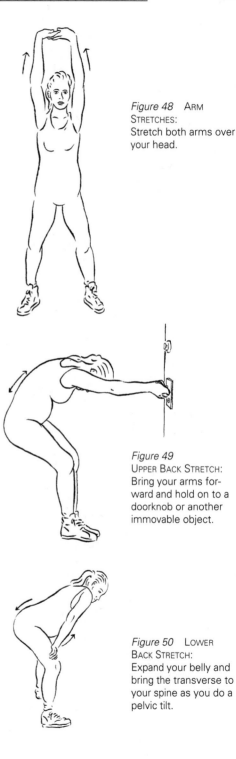

Figure 48 ARM STRETCHES: Stretch both arms over your head.

Figure 49 UPPER BACK STRETCH: Bring your arms forward and hold on to a doorknob or another immovable object.

Figure 50 LOWER BACK STRETCH: Expand your belly and bring the transverse to your spine as you do a pelvic tilt.

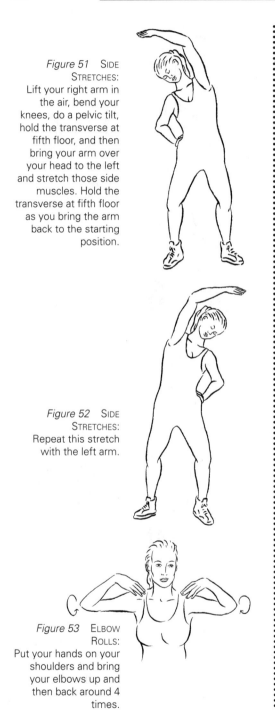

Figure 51 SIDE STRETCHES: Lift your right arm in the air, bend your knees, do a pelvic tilt, hold the transverse at fifth floor, and then bring your arm over your head to the left and stretch those side muscles. Hold the transverse at fifth floor as you bring the arm back to the starting position.

Figure 52 SIDE STRETCHES: Repeat this stretch with the left arm.

Figure 53 ELBOW ROLLS: Put your hands on your shoulders and bring your elbows up and then back around 4 times.

you roll up from the base of your spine one vertebra at a time.

Next we're going to do some *side stretches* (see Figures 51 and 52). We always stretch out the upper and lower back first, before we do them. So raise your right arm straight up in the air, bend your knees, give me a pelvic tilt to support your lower back, and hold that transverse at fifth floor as you move your arm over your head to the left. Now expand your belly and bring that transverse to the spine as you stretch those side muscles. Feel them lengthening. Now hold that transverse in on the work of bringing your arm back up to the starting position.

Now let's stretch out your other side. Raise your left arm straight up in the air, bend your knees, give me a pelvic tilt, and hold that transverse at fifth floor as you move your arm over your head to the right. Now expand your belly and bring that transverse to the spine as you feel those side muscles lengthening. Hold that transverse at fifth floor on the work of bringing your arm back to the starting position.

Let's warm up your shoulders with some *shoulder rolls*. If you're standing, remember to keep your knees loose to take the strain off your lower back. Don't let them lock. (If you have trouble standing, you can do the rest of these exercises sitting down.) Bring your shoulders up toward your ears and then back and then down, feeling those chest muscles lengthening and those upper back muscles shortening. We'll do 4 shoulder rolls.

Now put your hands on your shoulders and bring your elbows up and then back and around for 4 *elbow rolls* (see Figure 53). This circular movement is another exercise to lengthen those chest muscles. Next, hold your arms straight out to the sides and make like a *windmill* (see Figure 54) by bringing your arms down and then across each other, then up over your head and straight out to the sides. Let's do 2 of these. Again, feel those chest muscles lengthening.

Let's do *head and neck stretches*. Turn your head toward your right shoulder and then back to the center. Now toward your left shoulder and back to the center. If you're standing, remember to keep your knees soft and loose. Bring your chin to your chest and back to center. Tilt your head back to look up at the ceiling, then bring it back to the center. Be careful not to bring your head too far back. Now let's do some *neck stretches* (see Figures 55 and 56). Put your left hand on the right side of your head, gently move your head toward your left shoulder, and feel the right side of your neck lengthening. Slowly return to the center. Put your right hand on the left side of your head, gently move your head toward your right shoulder, and feel the lengthening in the left side of your neck.

Let's do one forward *head roll* from shoulder to shoulder, then one going back in the other direction, being careful not to drop your head too far back. Now to help with your posture, let's do some *chin-backs* (see Figure 57). Bring your chin straight back—like a turkey—and then relax. Try not to let your head fall forward. Feel how this movement brings your shoulders back and adjusts your posture?

Hold your hands straight out in front of you and let's do some *wrist circles* (see Figure 58), 4 in one direction, then 4 in the other direction. Remember to keep those knees soft if you're standing. By the way, swivel your wrists in the morning if you wake up with any numbness in your fingers.

Let's warm up your *waist* with some nice, easy fluid movements. If you've done the previous few warm-ups sitting down, now's the time to stand up

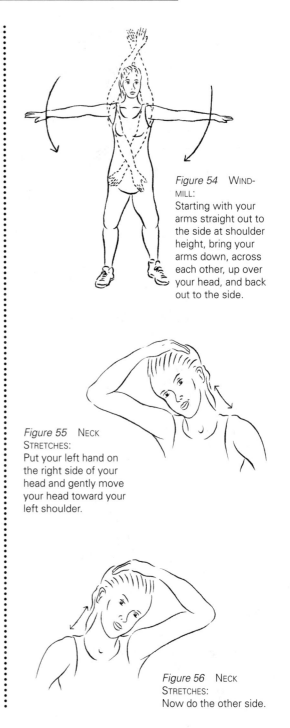

Figure 54 WIND-MILL: Starting with your arms straight out to the side at shoulder height, bring your arms down, across each other, up over your head, and back out to the side.

Figure 55 NECK STRETCHES: Put your left hand on the right side of your head and gently move your head toward your left shoulder.

Figure 56 NECK STRETCHES: Now do the other side.

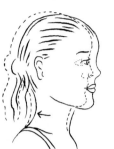

Figure 57   CHIN-BACKS:
Bring your chin straight
back like a turkey, and
then relax.

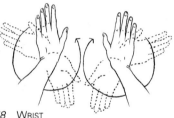

Figure 58   WRIST
CIRCLES:
Hold your hands
straight out in front of
you and do 4 wrist cir-
cles in each direction.

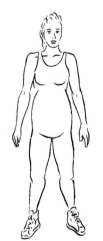

Figure 59   WAIST
STRETCHES:
(1) Bend your knees
and hold your hands
out to the side.

again. Bend your knees and hold your hands slightly out to the sides (see Figure 59). Turn your body to the right, lifting your left heel off the floor (see Figure 60). Now gently swing back to center (see Figure 59 again) and then to the left side, raising your right heel off the floor (see Figure 61). Do not lift foot completely off floor. Do this side-to-side movement 3 or 4 times.

Face front again, and let's do our standing *pelvic tilt* (see Figure 62). Knees bent, back flat, check that lower back by putting your hand on the small of your back. Now bring the bottom of your pelvis forward as you feel those lower back muscles lengthening. Hold to the count of 5, and then flatten your back again. You must bend your knees to move that pelvis. Now do some *hip circles* (see Figure 63), moving your pelvis forward and to one side, back and to the other side in a continuous flowing movement. Do this movement again in the other direction.

Time to warm up the *backs of your legs* (see Figure 64). Do touches and flexes with your right foot, touching your heel to the floor, then touching the ball of your foot to the floor. Do 4 of these. Don't point your toes; that can bring on leg cramps. Remember to flex your foot if you get a cramp in the middle of the night! Now do some *ankle circles* (see Figure 65). Circle the foot at the ankle in one direction for 4 circles and then in the other direction for 4 circles. Let's do the same routine with your left foot: heel and ball of your foot 4 times and then 4 foot circles.

Give a little attention to your *feet.* You'll probably get a little flat-footed during your pregnancy, and these exercises really help when your feet start hurting. So let's start with *knuckle presses* (see Figure 66). Press the bottom of the first knuckle of all of your

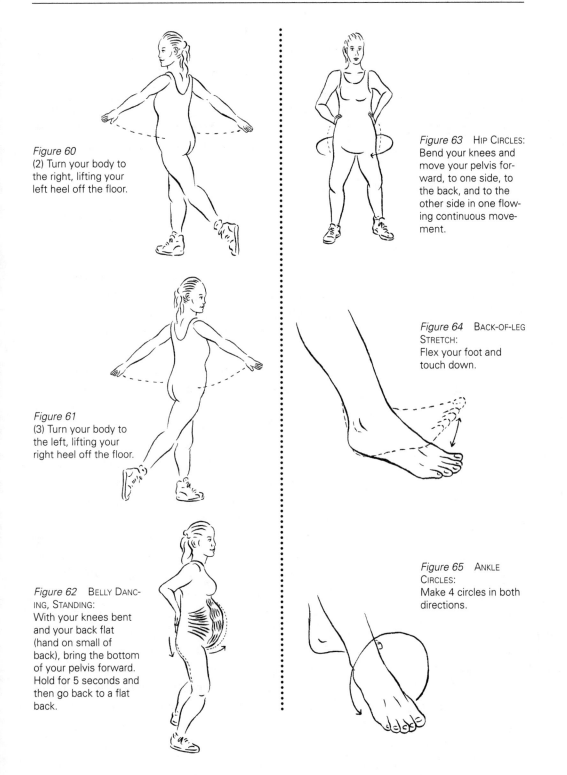

Figure 60
(2) Turn your body to the right, lifting your left heel off the floor.

Figure 61
(3) Turn your body to the left, lifting your right heel off the floor.

Figure 62 BELLY DANCING, STANDING:
With your knees bent and your back flat (hand on small of back), bring the bottom of your pelvis forward. Hold for 5 seconds and then go back to a flat back.

Figure 63 HIP CIRCLES:
Bend your knees and move your pelvis forward, to one side, to the back, and to the other side in one flowing continuous movement.

Figure 64 BACK-OF-LEG STRETCH:
Flex your foot and touch down.

Figure 65 ANKLE CIRCLES:
Make 4 circles in both directions.

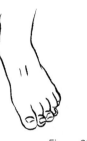

Figure 66 KNUCKLE
PRESS:
Press the first knuckles
of all of your toes into
the floor, and then
release.

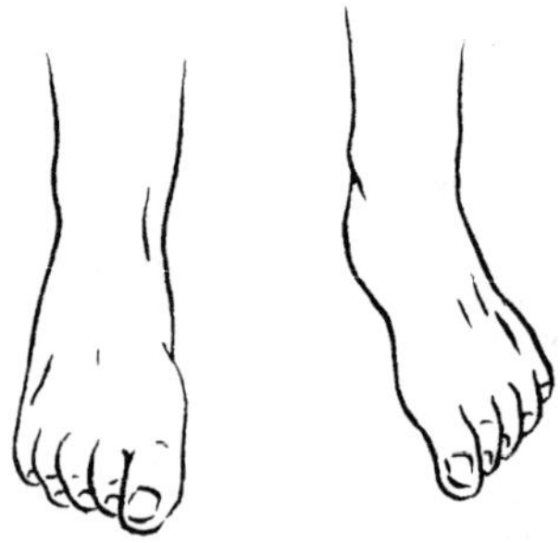

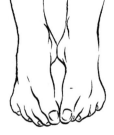

Figure 67 INCHWORM:
Curl all of your toes
back toward your
heels.

Figure 68 LITTLE O'S:
With your big toes and
your heels touching,
make a little o
between your feet.

toes into the floor and release. Do it once again. Now curl those toes up like an *inchworm* (see Figure 67), and really feel it in the arches of your feet. Once again. Now put your feet together so that your big toes and the insides of your heels are touching. Now make a *little O* (see Figure 68) in the middle by leaning your feet out to the sides. Do it once again.

Hands and Knees

The muscles in your groin area (hip flexors) tend to get very short during pregnancy due to the postural changes. Stretching these muscles out is important to help prevent lower back aches during pregnancy. So let's do the *runner's stretch* (see Figure 69). Get down on all fours. Now bring your right leg forward and place your right foot on the floor. Make sure your knee is lined up above your instep. Both hands are on the inside of this foot. Now slide the left leg back as far as you can and make sure your left foot is in a flexed position on the floor, and lean into the stretch. Hold the transverse at fifth floor as you slowly straighten your left knee (it will come 3 to 4 inches off the floor) and hold this position for 20 counts, if you can. Do not arch your back. Now lower your knee back to the floor. (For a *modification* of this exercise, see Figure 70. While doing exercises on all fours, remember: if you have problems with your wrists do not put your palms on the floor; instead, put your fists on the floor. Also, a pillow under your knee will be helpful if you have knee problems.)

Now hold on to something stable with your left hand as you straighten your back and your right knee. Let's stretch out the *back of your leg* (see Figure 71). Flex your right foot 4 times and bring it back toward you, feeling the stretch in the back of that right leg. Now bring your right leg back to its starting position, lean forward, and place your hands on the floor so you are again on all fours.

Let's do the runner's stretch on the other leg. Bring your left leg forward. Remember to line the knee up above your instep. Now slide your right leg back as far as you can and lean into the stretch. Keep that right foot in a flexed position. Now hold the transverse at fifth floor as you slowly straighten your right knee so that it rises off the floor, and hold this position for twenty seconds. Now put that right knee back on the mat. Hold on to something stable as you straighten your back and extend your left leg out in front of you. Flex your left foot 4 times, feeling that stretch in the back of your left leg. Now bring your left leg back to its starting position and return to all fours. The runner's stretch should really feel good on your back.

Let's continue our routine while you're still down there on all fours. Let's do our *pelvic tilt on all fours* (see Figure 72). Keeping a nice flat back and feet in a flexed position, think of a string pulling your tailbone down and moving the bottom of your pelvis forward. Hold it to the count of 5, and then flatten your back. Do not move your upper back; that will shorten your chest muscles. Remember, this is a small movement in your lower back. So let's do 10 of these pelvic tilts, and please use the transverse as you lengthen those lower back muscles.

Now we'll do another *side stretch*. Move your buttocks to the right side, and then look around over your right shoulder (see Figure 73). You should feel the stretch along the left side of your body. Now move your buttocks to the left and look

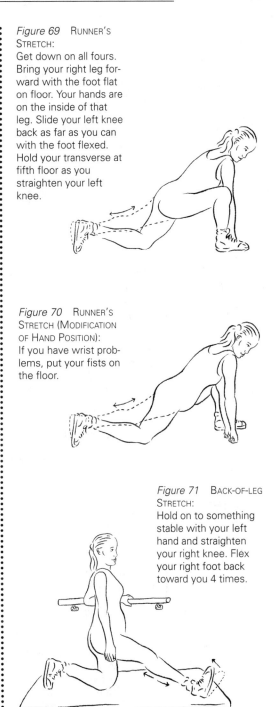

Figure 69 RUNNER'S STRETCH:
Get down on all fours. Bring your right leg forward with the foot flat on floor. Your hands are on the inside of that leg. Slide your left knee back as far as you can with the foot flexed. Hold your transverse at fifth floor as you straighten your left knee.

Figure 70 RUNNER'S STRETCH (MODIFICATION OF HAND POSITION):
If you have wrist problems, put your fists on the floor.

Figure 71 BACK-OF-LEG STRETCH:
Hold on to something stable with your left hand and straighten your right knee. Flex your right foot back toward you 4 times.

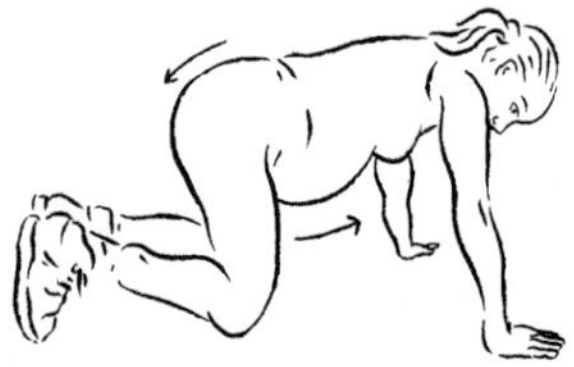

Figure 72   BELLY DANC-
ING, ON ALL FOURS:
Get down on all fours
with your back flat.
Bring the bottom of
your pelvis forward and
then back.

Figure 73   SIDE
STRETCH:
Move your buttocks to
the right side and then
look around over your
right shoulder.

Figure 74   SIDE
STRETCH:
Move your buttocks to
the left, and then look
around over your left
shoulder.

over your left shoulder (see Figure 74). Once again, feel the stretch.

We're ready for some *pregnancy push-ups,* to work the pectorals, or chest muscles. Starting position is on your hands and knees with your shoulders lined up over your wrists and your feet flexed on the floor behind you. Now, bend your arms and slowly lower your forehead so that it is touching the floor, slightly above your hands. The transverse is always at fifth floor on the work part of the exercise, and in this exercise the work occurs when you straighten your arms. When you're bringing the transverse to fifth, you're also counting, or exhaling. So let's do it. In the starting position, with your forehead on the floor, expand your belly (see Figure 75). Now take your transverse to fifth as you straighten your arms and say "one" (see Figure 76). Now expand your belly on your way back down as your forehead touches the floor. Now bring the transverse to the spine as you straighten your arms and count "two." Remember to keep your upper back straight as you come up. If you curve your upper back you are shortening the chest muscles. Aim for 10 push-ups to start with, and work up to four sets of 20.

We're going to wrap up our hands-and-knees exercises by doing some *elevators.* Take a belly breath and expand your belly, and then bring your belly button back to your spine (see Figure 76 again). Hold the transverse there at fifth floor for a count of 30. Now close your eyes and see that belly button going out the back of your spine to sixth floor for 5 counts as you press that belly button back. Now end with another belly breath. Expand your belly as you take air in through your nose and exhale through your mouth as you bring your belly button back to your spine.

Now stand up. Remember how to do it? Put your right leg forward with your hand above your right knee; now bring your left leg forward and put your hand above your left knee. This puts you in the hands-above-knees position we learned while doing the pelvic tilt. Hold that transverse at fifth floor as you roll up from the base of the spine one vertebra at a time.

Now hold on to a doorjamb or a heavy piece of furniture and do your *squat* for three to five minutes (see Figure 77). *A word of caution:* If you have swollen veins in your pelvic area this may not be a good exercise to do.

Do some kegels while you're squatting. This is the hardest position to do them in, because all of your "groceries" are pressing on the pelvic floor muscles. When you get out of the squat, remember to sit down using one hand and then the other hand to help you down. Do not stand up from the squatting position—it's very hard on your knees and abdominals.

Seated Warm-Up

Let's sit down and do the last stretch that we learned in the BAKS Basics: the *backs-of-the-legs stretch*. Sit with one leg bent with that foot touching the inside of the other leg, which is straight. Make sure the foot of your straight leg is lined up with your thigh. Rest your hands below the knee of your straight leg (see Figure 78). Close your eyes. Soften that knee. Put your mind in your muscles and see the muscles running down the back of

Figure 75 PREGNANCY PUSH-UPS:
(1) In an on-all-fours position, put your forehead on the floor and take a belly breath.

Figure 76
(2) Bring the transverse to fifth floor as you straighten your arms and exhale, counting out loud.

Figure 77 SUPPORTED SQUAT:
Hold on to an immovable object with your arms straight at shoulder height, your heels on the floor, and your weight shifted to the outsides of your feet. Hold for 15 to 20 seconds. Work up to 5 minutes 5 times a day.

Figure 78 STRETCHING THE BACKS OF YOUR LEGS: (1) Sit on the floor with one leg straight, foot lined up with thigh, and one leg bent, foot resting against the opposite knee. Your hands are below the straight knee. Relax that knee and the back of that leg. Now expand your belly.

Figure 79 (2) Bring the transverse to fifth floor and exhale as you bring your hands toward your feet. Hold for 10 to 20 seconds. Keeping the transverse at fifth floor, roll up from the base of the spine one vertebra at a time.

Figure 80 AB ELEVATORS: (1) Sit cross-legged with one hand on your belly, one hand on your back, and your back supported. Take a belly breath, bring the transverse to fifth floor, and hold it there for 30 counts.

your leg relaxing. We always relax a muscle before we stretch it. Now let's breathe through the stretch. Expand the belly, then bring the transverse to the spine and *hold* it there as you slide your hands down your extended leg, stretching forward gently as far as you can go. See the muscles behind your leg lengthen (see Figure 79). One more time. Expand the belly, transverse to the spine, *hold* it there as you bring your hands forward even more and see those muscles lengthen. Now hold the transverse at fifth floor on the work of straightening your back one vertebra at a time from the base of your spine. Now repeat this exercise on the other leg.

Next, move over to a wall and do the transverse part of the Tupler Technique (breathing the right way, working a strengthened transverse muscle, and relaxing a strengthened PC muscle). Sit cross-legged with your back against a wall, one hand on your belly, and one hand on your back, or sit in a chair if you prefer. The first exercise is the *elevator*. Take a belly breath and expand your belly. Now bring the transverse to fifth floor and *hold* it there as you count to 30 (see Figure 80). Don't worry about your breathing. If you're counting, you're exhaling, and if you're exhaling, you're breathing. Now close your eyes and see that belly button pulsing out the back, or through sixth floor, for 5 counts (see Figure 81). Use your hand to feel that motion in your back. Remember, only the belly button moves—no shoulders, back, or leg movements.

Now let's end the exercise with a belly breath. Expand your belly as you take air in through your nose and exhale through your mouth as you bring your belly back to your spine. Relax for a moment.

Let's do the second transverse exercise, the *contracting* (see Figure 82). Sit the same way, with one hand on your belly and one hand on your back. Take a belly breath and then bring your belly button to third floor, which is halfway between first and fifth. This is our starting position. Now bring your belly button to fifth floor and then release it just a little to third floor and then back to fifth floor. Hold the position briefly on the backward movement at fifth floor. Do 100 squeezes from third to fifth floor as you count out loud. If you have practiced contracting for a week with the BAKS Basics, you should be able to do 100. Count out loud. If you're counting, you're exhaling, and if you're exhaling, you're breathing.

If you get out of breath doing this transverse work or if the breathing isn't working easily, count slower. When the muscle gets stronger, make the movement smaller. Do the movement from fourth to fifth floor. When the muscle gets even stronger, do the exercise fifth to sixth floor, as in the elevator exercise. Remember, every time you bring the transverse back, you shorten the recti from the middle and you bring it closer together. These two exercises can also be done using a scarf or sheet as a splint to support the two halves of the recti muscle (see Figure 83).

Figure 81
(2) Still holding transverse at fifth floor, bring the belly button out the back to sixth floor for 5 little pulses. Keep counting out loud. Do 10 sets of 5 pulses.

Figure 82
AB CONTRACTING:
Bring the belly button to third floor (halfway between first and fifth). Now pulse back to fifth floor, hold it there a moment as you count out loud. The emphasis is on holding at fifth floor. One set is 100 third-to-fifth-floor pulses. Do 5 sets a day.

Upper Body Workout

Now we're ready to work the upper body. Let's do some exercises to shorten the upper back muscles and strengthen the shoulders. Make sure your light weights and Dyna-Band are handy.

Let's do a little stretching of the upper body first. You should be sitting cross-legged, but you'll want

Figure 83   SPLINTING THE RECTI:
Bring the two halves of the rectus abdominis together with a sheet or long scarf and hold it there while you are doing transverse abdominal work.

Figure 84 Upper Body
Stretch I (Right):
(1) Lift your right arm in
an L shape, your elbow
in line with your shoul-
der. Grasp that elbow
with your left hand and
pull the elbow toward
your head.

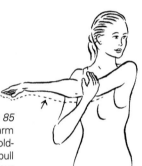

Figure 85
(2) Bring your right arm
in front of you, still holding the elbow, and pull
it gently across your
body as you look over
your right shoulder.

Figure 86 Upper Body
Stretch (Left):
(1) Lift your left arm in
an L shape, keeping
your elbow in line with
your shoulder. Grasp
that elbow with your
right hand and pull the
elbow toward your
head.

to move out from the wall so you can get your arms behind you. Lift your right arm in an L shape with your elbow in line with your shoulder; grasp your right elbow with your left hand and pull it back toward your head (see Figure 84). Now bring your right arm in front of you, still holding the elbow, and pull it gently across your body as you look over your right shoulder (see Figure 85).

Stretch out that left arm: elbow in line with the shoulder, pull it back toward your head with your right arm (see Figure 86). Bring your arm in front of you and pull it across your body as you look over your left shoulder (see Figure 87).

Clasp your hands behind your back. Keeping your chin down, bring your shoulders back and stretch out those chest muscles. Feels good across your chest, right? Now with your hands still clasped behind you, lift them up in the air. Bring them back down and relax (see Figure 88).

Let's start our upper body workout with the *military press*. It's best to do this exercise without handheld weights until you can coordinate the exercise with the transverse work. It's a little diffi-cult at first to work two parts of your body at the same time. Bring your arms out to the sides in a 45-degree angle with your elbows below your shoul-ders (see Figure 89). Expand the belly, now bring the transverse to fifth floor as you straighten your arms above your head and count "one" (see Figure 90). Remember not to lock your elbows. We do slow, controlled movements. Now bring the arms back to the starting position, keeping that trans-verse at fifth floor.

Do 8 to 10 military presses (one set) ending each set with a belly breath. Start with two sets and work up to four sets. Make sure when you're working the transverse that you do not move or round your lower back. Only the belly button moves. It's easy to cheat and move that lower back. When your transverse becomes stronger, start the exercise at fifth floor and then bring it to sixth floor as you lift your arms over your head. When you can comfortably do four sets of 15 repetitions, start doing the presses using your weights if you wish. Start light and slowly work your way up to no more than 5 pounds. This exercise is not good to do, especially with weights, if you have shoulder problems.

The next exercise for your shoulders is the *table tops*. Bring your arms out to your sides in an L position, your shoulders lined up with your elbows and your elbows lined up with your wrists (see Figure 91). Expand your belly. Bring the transverse to fifth floor as you raise your elbows to shoulder height and count "one" (see Figure 92). Keep that transverse at fifth floor as you return your arms to the starting position. Work up to four sets of 15 repetitions. Then start using weights if you wish. Remember to end each set with a belly breath. Start with two sets of 10. As your transverse gets stronger, you can do this exercise working the transverse, as in the military press.

Grab your Dyna-Band and let's do some *forward pulls* (see Figure 93). Still sitting cross-legged, hold your arms out in front of you a little past your shoulders at chest height, palms facing each other. Hold the ends of the band in your hands. Take a belly breath, get that transverse to the spine, and hold it there as you pull your hands apart until the band is touching your chest. Now, keeping your arms nice and straight but not locking your elbows, palms facing forward, move your arms back behind your shoulders to the count of 5. The transverse should be moving in the same backward direction as the arms (fifth to sixth). It's important to keep your back

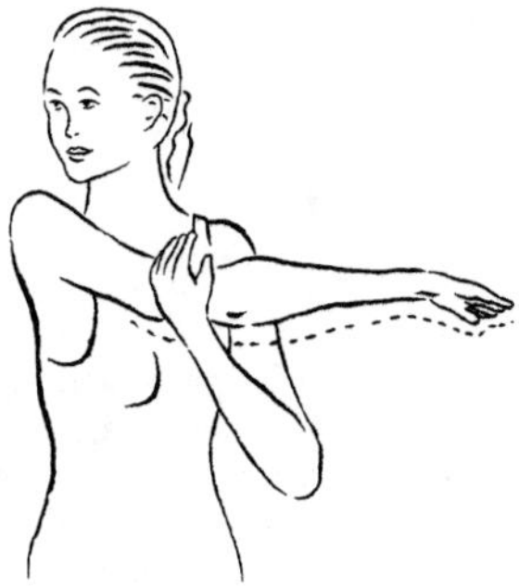

Figure 87
(2) Bring your left arm in front of you, still holding the elbow, and pull it gently across your body as you look over your left shoulder.

Figure 88   UPPER BODY STRETCH II:
Clasp your hands behind your back. Keeping your chin down, bring your shoulders back and stretch out your chest muscles. Now lift your clasped hands in the air.

Figure 89   MILITARY PRESS:
(1) Hold your arms out to the side at a 45-degree angle, keeping your elbows below your shoulders.

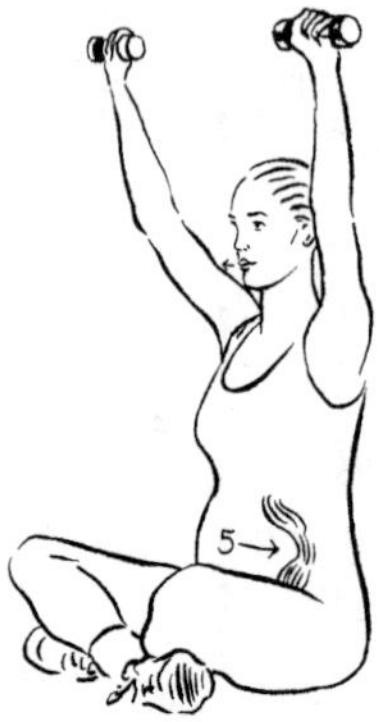

Figure 90
(2) Bring the transverse to fifth floor as you straighten your arms above your head and exhale, counting out loud.

Figure 91   TABLETOPS:
(1) Bring your arms out to your sides in an L position, your shoulders lined up with your elbows and your elbows lined up with your wrists. Take a belly breath.

Figure 92
(2) Bring the transverse to fifth floor as you raise your elbows to shoulder height and exhale, counting out loud.

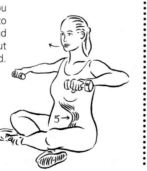

Figure 93   FORWARD PULLS:
Sit cross-legged while holding the ends of the Dyna-Band out in front of you. Pull your arms apart until the band is touching your chest. Take a belly breath and bring the transverse to fifth floor. Hold it there. Now bring your transverse to sixth floor as you move your arms behind your shoulders.

Figure 94
You should feel this forward pull exercise between your shoulder blades.

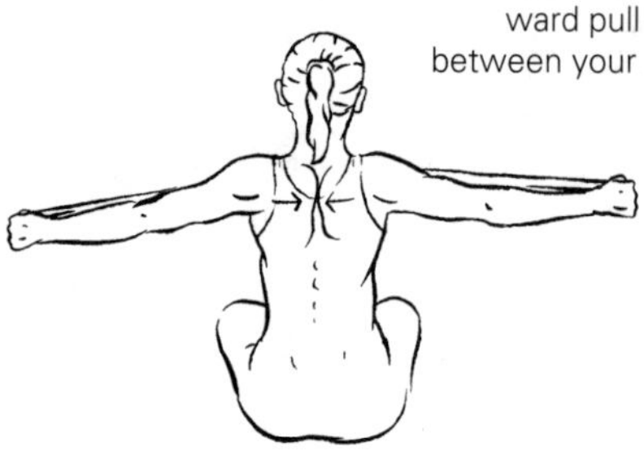

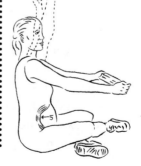

Figure 95   UPS AND DOWNS:
Holding the ends of the band with your arms straight out in front of you, raise the arms up to your ears. The transverse stays at fifth floor during this whole exercise.

flat. It's easy to arch your back while doing this exercise, but if you do that, you can't work your transverse muscle. If you can't do fifth to sixth, then just hold it at fifth floor. Do 5 repetitions. Keep the band on your chest the whole time. You should feel this exercise between your shoulder blades (see Figure 94). The stronger you get, the tighter or shorter you can make the band for more resistance. Work up to four sets of 10 repetitions. Remember to take a belly breath after each set.

Now still holding the ends of the band with straight arms, let's do some *ups and downs* (see Figure 95). Raise your arms over your head so that your upper arms are beside your ears. Remember, make slow, controlled movements. Don't strain your shoulders. Don't pull your arms behind your ears. Now bring your arms back to the starting position. Hold the transverse at fifth floor during the whole exercise. This is not a good exercise if you have shoulder problems.

Now, keep holding either end of your Dyna-Band and do some *overhead pulls*. Both your arms are straight over your head with your palms facing each other. Adjust the band. Make it longer for less resistance (easier) or shorter for more resistance (harder). Take a belly breath. Holding your transverse at fifth floor, pull your hands apart until they are level with the top of your head (see Figure 96). Palms are now facing forward. (This is the starting position.) Now bring the transverse to sixth floor while you pull the band down behind the head to shoulder height (see Figure 97). Release the band slowly to the starting position, taking that transverse back to fifth floor. Then go back to sixth as you bring the band back down.

This movement reminds me of a bird flying, so keep your wings straight as you're doing this exer-

Figure 96 OVERHEAD PULLS:
(1) Holding both ends of your Dyna-Band and holding your transverse at fifth floor, pull your hands apart until they are level with the top of your head.

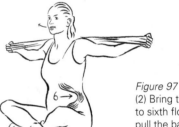

Figure 97
(2) Bring the transverse to sixth floor while you pull the band to shoulder height, keeping the band behind your head.

Figure 98 LAT PULL-DOWNS:
(1) Shorten the Dyna-Band. Hold your hands out to the sides below ear level (same starting position as the military press) and expand your belly.

Figure 99
(2) Bring the transverse to fifth floor as you lower your elbows to your sides and exhale, counting out loud.

Figure 100   ROWING: (1) Wrap the Dyna-Band around your feet, holding one end in each hand. Expand your belly and hold the transverse at fifth floor.

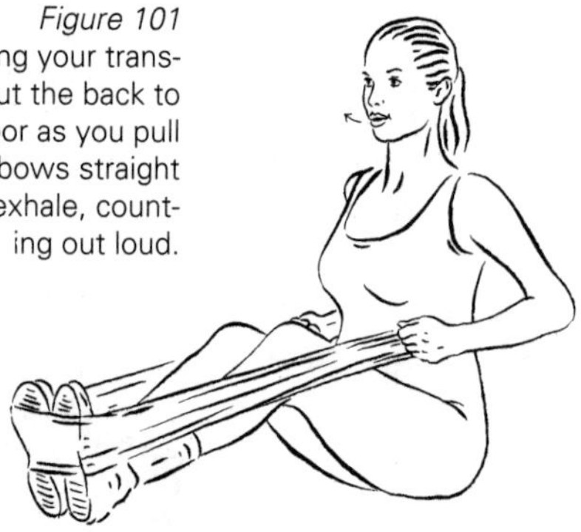

Figure 101
(2) Bring your transverse out the back to sixth floor as you pull your elbows straight back and exhale, counting out loud.

cise! Elbows are straight but not locked. The movement is from under your arms. Remember to make slow, controlled movements so that you work the muscles effectively and safely. Start with 10 repetitions or as many as you can do. Work up to four sets of 20 repetitions, ending each set with a belly breath. Again, you should be feeling this in your upper back. Keep the resistance in the Dyna-Band during the whole exercise. When you get stronger, give yourself more resistance by shortening the band.

The next exercise is the *lat pull-down*. Make the Dyna-Band shorter now, still holding the ends of the Dyna-Band. Your hands should be out to the sides just below ear level, in the same starting position as the military press (see Figure 98). Palms are facing forward. I want your head, neck, and spine all in a nice vertical line—no leaning forward or looking down at your belly, because that brings your shoulders forward and throws your alignment off. Now expand the belly and take your transverse to the spine as you bring your elbows down to your sides and count "one" (see Figure 99). The Dyna-Band is behind you during this exercise. Keep your belly at fifth floor as you bring your elbows back to the starting position. In this exercise it's really hard *not* to arch your back. Remember, if you do arch your back you are shortening your lower back muscles, and that makes it hard to work the transverse muscle. Start with 8 repetitions or as many as you can do. Work up to four sets of 15 to 20 repetitions. Remember to take a belly breath after each set and to keep the resistance in the band the whole time. When your transverse becomes stronger you can start the exercise at fifth floor and then bring it to sixth floor on the work.

We'll end our upper body work with a little *rowing*. Still sitting with a nice flat back, bring your legs in front of you, knees bent. Wrap your Dyna-Band around your feet, holding one end in each hand, elbows bent and lined up below your shoulders, palms facing each other (see Figure 100).

Expand the belly, get that belly button to fifth floor, *hold* it there, and then bring it to sixth floor as you pull your elbows straight back and count "one" (see Figure 101). Feel those shoulder blades coming together. Stay at fifth floor as you move the elbows back to the starting position. Try not to let the elbows go forward of the shoulder, as this shortens the chest muscles. Again, remember not to arch your back. Do 10 rowing moves, or as many as you can do. Work up to four sets of 20 repetitions. Remember, nothing moves except the arms and the belly button.

If you do your upper body exercises regularly, your upper back and shoulders will feel much better.

Legs I

Now we're going to move down and strengthen your leg muscles. First we'll do one leg, break the workout up in the middle with some abdominal work; then we'll do the other leg.

During all of these side-lying leg exercises, I want you to put your free hand on your belly. That's a good place to store it, for one thing, and it's a great way to check that you're taking belly breaths and working your transverse.

Lie on your left side on the mat and get ready to do some *leg circles* (see Figure 102). With your head resting on your arm or pillow, your left leg bent, and

Figure 102
LEG CIRCLES:
Lie on your side with your bottom leg bent and your top leg straight. Keep your transverse at fifth floor while you make big circles with your top leg.

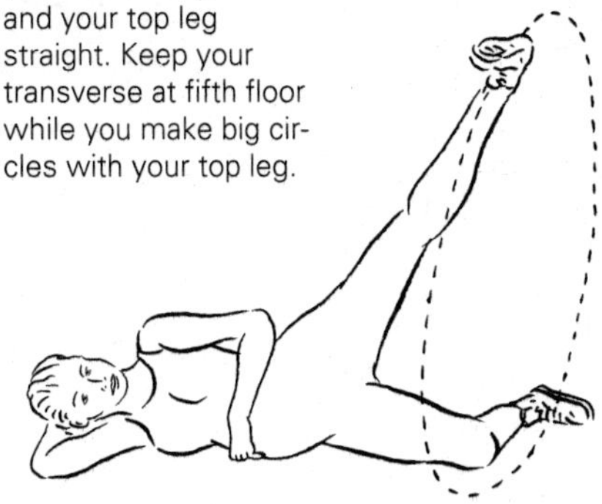

Figure 103   OYSTERS:
(1) Lie on your side with your legs bent, feet flexed, legs together, one hand on belly, and transverse at fifth floor.

Figure 104
(2) Bring the transverse out the back to sixth floor as you lift your top leg, knee facing forward, and exhale, counting out loud. Bring the transverse to fifth floor as you lower the leg.

Figure 105
STRAIGHT-BEND OYSTERS:
(1) Start in the same
starting position as the
oyster.

Figure 106
(2) Keeping the trans-
verse at fifth floor,
straighten the top leg.

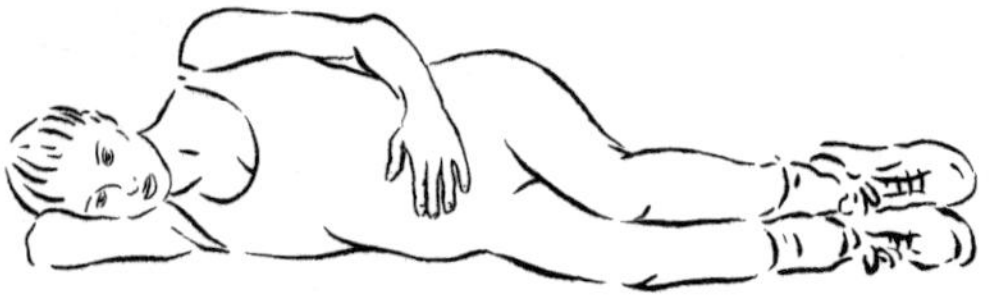

Figure 107
(3) Keeping the trans-
verse at fifth floor,
bend the top leg and
bring it back to the
starting position.

your right leg straight, take a belly breath, bring your transverse to the spine, and hold it there as you make big circles with your top leg. Think of making an *O* shape, 4 in one direction and 4 in the other. Remember to make slow, controlled movements.

The next exercise is called the *oyster*. It's great for preventing that pregnant waddle and for strengthening the outer thigh muscles. Strong legs are really helpful during labor.

Still lying on your left side with your head supported by your arm, keep those knees bent, feet flexed and legs together (see Figure 103). Expand the belly, bring the transverse to fifth floor, hold it there, and then go out the back, to sixth floor as you lift your entire right leg as one unit with the knee facing forward. Lift it about three inches and count "one" (see Figure 104). Have you got your right hand on your belly, feeling that transverse move back as you lift your leg? Bring the belly button back to fifth floor as you return your leg to the starting position. Let's count off 20 little oyster lifts, each time squeezing that belly button back from fifth to sixth floor. Now bring the top knee forward to touch the floor and release the outer thigh muscle. Time to rest that leg.

While you're resting, relax those abdominals, hold that PC muscle in and do a kegel for the count of 10. We want to learn to use the transverse muscle and the pelvic floor muscles separately, because when you're in labor pushing, the transverse muscle is tight and the pelvic floor muscles are open and relaxed. The only time you hold them in together is when you sneeze or cough.

This leg lift should be a small motion, like a small oyster opening. Remember, raise your leg only about three inches. The knee should be pointing forward, not shooting up in the air. By keeping the knee facing forward you'll work the muscle, not the joint. Your leg should be lifting all at once—so flat you could balance a cup of water on it. Work up to three sets of 20 repetitions. Do a set of kegels and take a belly breath in between each set.

Let's do some *straight-bend oysters*. Start out in the same position as with the oyster, lying on your left side, knees bent and legs together (see Figure 105). Now straighten your top leg (see Figure 106). Then return it to the bent position and do an oyster lift (see Figures 107 and 108). So you straighten, bend, and lift. Again, start with a belly breath, bring that transverse to the spine, and *hold* it there at fifth as you straighten and then bend the leg. Bring it to sixth floor as you do the oyster lift and say "one." Let's do 10 of these. Now bring your top knee forward to touch the floor and release that muscle we've been working. Rest. Now relax those abdominals, hold that PC muscle in, and do a kegel for the count of 10. Work up to three sets of 20 repetitions of this exercise. Do a set of kegels in between each set.

Now we'll do a series of *side-lying adductions,* which are leg lifts to strengthen the inner thigh, or adductor, muscles. You're still lying on your left side, head supported by your arm, and your top leg is bent at the knee. Relax that top leg and rest it in front of you on the floor or prop it up on a pillow for support, if that feels better. The illustrations show this exercise done with a supporting pillow. Now straighten your bottom leg so that it's in line with your torso (see Figure 109). Rest your top arm on your belly and not on the floor; I don't want you using the arm to help lift the leg.

The first exercise is the *ups and downs*. Expand the belly and then bring your belly button to fifth floor and hold it there as you lift that bottom leg as

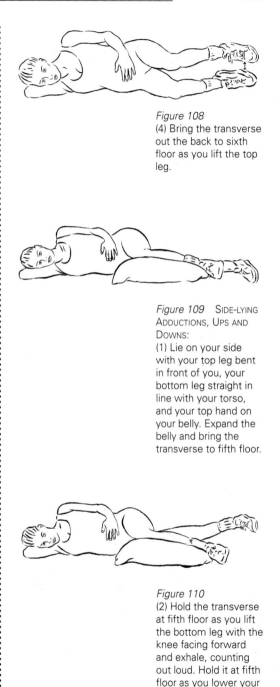

Figure 108
(4) Bring the transverse out the back to sixth floor as you lift the top leg.

Figure 109   SIDE-LYING ADDUCTIONS, UPS AND DOWNS:
(1) Lie on your side with your top leg bent in front of you, your bottom leg straight in line with your torso, and your top hand on your belly. Expand the belly and bring the transverse to fifth floor.

Figure 110
(2) Hold the transverse at fifth floor as you lift the bottom leg with the knee facing forward and exhale, counting out loud. Hold it at fifth floor as you lower your leg to the floor.

Figure 111 SIDE-LYING
ADDUCTIONS, LITTLE
LIFTS:
Your transverse goes
from fifth to sixth floor
as you do 10 little lifts
with the bottom leg.

Figure 112 SIDE-LYING
ADDUCTION,
MODIFICATION:
(1)

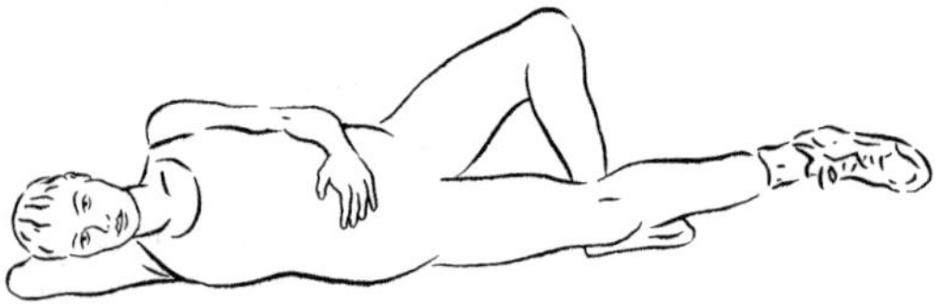

Figure 113 SIDE-LYING
ADDUCTION,
MODIFICATION:
(2)

high as possible, exhale, and say "one" (see Figure 110). Think of your transverse lifting that leg, your transverse doing all the work! Keep your knee facing forward and the foot flexed while you're lifting the leg. Now slowly lower your leg to the floor, keeping your transverse at fifth floor. This is an up-and-down movement. Make sure your leg touches the floor each time. Let's do a set of 10 lifts, each one starting with a belly breath so the transverse will be in the right starting position and will be in on the work of the lift.

When you're doing side-lying adductions if you feel it in your lower back, bring the leg you're lifting slightly forward for the starting position of your next repetition.

The next exercise is a *hold.* You simply hold that bottom leg in the air for 10 counts. Lie on your left side in the same starting position you used in the ups and downs (see Figure 109). Take a belly breath, transverse to the spine, and hold it there as you lift your bottom leg in the air. Hold your leg steady and keep your transverse at fifth floor as you exhale and count to 10 (see Figure 110). Lower the leg to the floor, holding the transverse at fifth floor.

The final exercise is a series of *little lifts* as you keep the leg in the air. While lying on your left side (see Figure 109), expand your belly and bring the transverse to fifth floor as you lift the bottom leg. This time your transverse goes from fifth to sixth floor as you do 10 little lifts (see Figure 111). Make sure you keep you hand on your belly so you can feel it moving back as you do these little lifts. Are you ready? Expand the belly, take your transverse to the spine as you lift your leg. Are you at fifth floor? Good. *Hold* it there as you do little lifts and bring that transverse from fifth to sixth with each little lift as you exhale and say "one." Count to 10. Now slowly lower your leg to the floor as you keep that transverse at fifth floor.

It's going to feel harder to work the transverse in this side-lying position. Relax, rest the abdominals, and hold that PC muscle in, and give me a kegel for the count of 10. When you've strengthened your inner thigh muscles a bit more, make this workout tougher by combining these three exercises without stopping in between. Work up to four sets of 30. Each set will include 10 up-and-down lifts, a ten-second hold in the air, and 10 more little lifts.

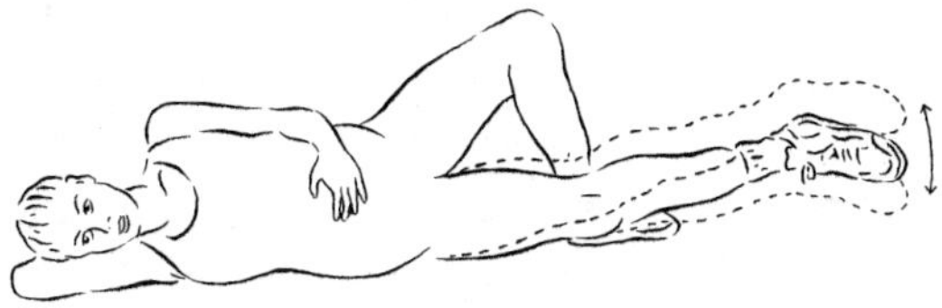

MODIFICATION: If you have not been exercising these muscles or have difficulty doing this exercise as directed, you can do all of the leg lifts with your top leg bent and positioned behind the bottom leg (see Figures 112, 113, and 114).

Figure 114   SIDE-LYING ADDUCTION, MODIFICATION: (3)

Back

Now we're going to do some abdominal and pelvic exercises, and these will give you a heavy-duty workout because you'll be doing them while lying on your back. The effects of gravity on the abdominal muscles make them harder to do in this position.

You're still lying on your side on the mat. Now roll over to your back without lifting your head. Remember what I've told you before: if you start feeling dizzy or queasy when you're on your back, just roll over onto your side and continue the exercise or do another exercise while lying on your side. In any case, I don't want you to be on your back for more than three or four minutes at a time without rolling to one side.

Figure 115   BACK-LYING TRANSVERSE CONTRACTING: With your knees bent, one hand on your belly, and one hand slightly under the small of your back, expand your belly and bring the transverse to fifth floor. Close your eyes and feel the transverse going out the back to sixth floor for 20 pulses as you count out loud.

We're going to do some *back-lying transverse contracting* (see Figure 115). If you've been keeping up with your BAKS routine on a daily basis and doing both transverse exercises (10 elevators a day and five sets of 100 contracting exercises a day) in a sitting position, by now you've developed the mind-body awareness as well as the strength to work your transverse in this harder supine position. It's important to learn to work the transverse muscle from fifth to sixth floor while lying on your back, because there is a strong possibility that's how you'll be using it when you're pushing during labor. Also, that's how you'll be using it when we get to the head lifts later in the workout.

Lie on your back with your knees comfortably bent and your feet flat on the floor. Put one hand on your belly and one hand slightly under your back. Put a pillow under your head if that feels more comfortable. Expand the belly and bring your transverse to fifth floor. Now close your eyes and see your transverse going out the back to sixth floor and touching your hand behind your back. Do 20 of these small pulses. Remember to count out loud so you don't hold your breath. Counting also helps you work the muscle while you're in this position. If you're counting out loud, you're exhaling, and if you're exhaling, you're breathing. End the exercise with a belly breath. Expand your belly, taking air in through your nose, and exhale through your mouth as you bring your belly back to your spine. Do 20 back-lying contracting exercises at least three times a day. Do them before or after you do your back-lying pelvic tilts (the next exercise). If you do more than one set of 20 repetitions, rest after each set and take a belly breath. As with all the back-lying exercises, if you feel light-headed or dizzy, roll to your side.

Now we're going to do the *back-lying pelvic tilt*. You learned this exercise in the BAKS Basics. This is the foundation of the head lift. You *must* have your transverse at fifth floor as you bring your pubic bone toward your navel. Most people release it when they do this movement. Remember not to use your legs or lift your buttocks off the mat, and always keep one hand on your belly and one hand under your back so you know you are working the transverse muscle in the right direction—back, not forward. In the same position—lying on the mat, knees bent, feet apart at hip distance and flat on the floor, one hand on your belly and one hand under your back—give me a belly breath as you expand the belly (see Figure 116), and bring the transverse to the spine (see Figure 117). Hold it there, as you bring your pubic bone toward your navel and exhale as you say "one" (see Figure 118). Now expand as you relax the pelvis and get ready to start the next pelvic tilt. Let's do 10 of these. We expand each time we do this exercise.

Legs II

Okay, let's finish off our leg work by exercising the left leg. To work the opposite leg, review Figures 102–111. You may also want to review the more detailed instructions for the leg exercises on pages 113–17. What follows is a quick run-through for the left leg, assuming you've already worked the right.

Roll onto your right side, remembering not to lift your head as you roll. Let's start doing *leg circles* with your left leg. Remember, the bottom leg is bent and the top one is straight. Take a belly breath, expand the belly, bring the transverse to the spine and hold it there as you make big circles with your leg, 4 one way and then 4 the other way.

Remember the *oyster?* Concentrate on little lifts. Knees are bent, legs are together, and feet are flexed. Keeping your knee pointing straight ahead, you're going to lift your top leg, keeping it straight. It's going to be so flat you could balance a cup on it. Keep your hand on your belly so you can feel that transverse working in a backward direction as you lift your leg. Remember that every time you work your transverse, you are shortening the recti from the middle.

Take a belly breath as you expand your belly, bring your transverse to fifth floor; hold it there as you lift the leg, feel that transverse going out the back, exhale, and say "one." Keep your transverse at fifth floor as you do the next lift. Do 20 oysters. End the exercise with a belly breath. Bring that top leg forward and down until it touches the floor. This will release the muscles we're working. While you're resting, relax those abdominals, hold that PC muscle in, and give me a kegel for a count of 10. Work up to three sets of 20 oysters.

Figure 116 BACK-LYING PELVIC TILT:
(1) With your knees bent, one hand on your belly, and one hand slightly under the small of your back, expand your belly.

Figure 117
(2) Now bring the transverse to fifth floor.

Figure 118
(3) Hold at fifth floor as you bring your pubic bone toward your navel and exhale, counting out loud.

Still lying on your right side, knees bent and legs together, you'll do some *straight-bend oysters*. Straighten your top leg, return it to the bent position resting on the bottom leg, and then do the oyster lift. Keep your hand on your belly so you can feel that transverse working. As always, start with a belly breath, expanding the belly and then bringing it to the spine; hold it at fifth floor as you straighten the leg, and keep it at fifth floor as you bend the leg. Then bring the transverse out the back to sixth floor as you do the oyster lift, exhale, and say "one." Stay at fifth floor as you start the next repetition. Let's do 10 of these. Now release the muscle by bringing the top leg forward so the knee is touching the floor. While you're resting, relax the abdominals and hold that PC muscle in as you give me a kegel for a count of 10. Work up to three sets of 20 repetitions.

Let's move on to the inner thigh exercises and *side-lying adductions*. Remember, you have two ways to do this exercise—with the top leg up (beginning shown in the modification) or down on pillow (more advanced). So straighten your bottom leg, making sure it's slightly in front of your body; if it's too far back, the exercise will stress your lower back.

Put your hand on your belly, take a belly breath, expand your belly, bring your transverse to your spine and hold it there as you lift the leg, exhale, and say "one." Remember to let that transverse muscle lift your leg. Lower the leg slowly to the floor, holding your transverse at fifth floor. Keep that foot flexed and that knee pointing forward. This is an up-and-down movement. Let's do 10 of these lifts.

The next exercise consists of holding that leg in the air for ten seconds. So expand your belly, bring your transverse to your spine and hold it there as you lift your leg and hold it in the air to the count of 10. Now slowly lower the leg back to the floor still holding that transverse at fifth floor.

In the final leg exercise you'll do little pulses as you keep the leg in the air. This time your transverse goes from fifth to sixth floor as you do the little lifts. Make sure you keep you hand on your belly so you can feel it moving back as you do these little lifts. Are you ready? Expand your belly and bring your transverse to your spine as you lift your leg. Is your transverse at fifth floor? Good. Hold it there as you do little lifts and bring that transverse from fifth to sixth with each little lift as you exhale and say "one." Count to 10. Now slowly lower the leg to the floor as you keep that transverse at fifth floor. Remember to end with a belly breath and a little kegeling. After you get the hang of coordinating the transverse and you get stronger, combine all three of these exercises. Work up to four sets of 30 repetitions.

Now that your leg muscles have had a good workout, we're going to go back to those abdominals one more time. We're going to do *head lifts*. Before you start them you should be able to do 100 repetitions of the contracting exercise at a time—transverse muscle from third to fifth floor—in a sitting position. If you're doing your five sets of 100 every day, you're probably strong enough. You should also be able to do the pelvic tilt correctly while lying on your back. That means your transverse is at fifth when you press your back to the floor. Remember, that's the foundation of the head lift. If you pass this test you are ready to do head lifts. Again, if you get light-headed or dizzy, remember to roll onto your side.

Give the recti muscle some external support when you do head lifts by wrapping a sheet or a long scarf around your middle and pulling the two ends across your belly to act as a splint. Lie on your back on the mat with your knees bent and your feet flat on the floor. Put the sheet or scarf underneath you by holding your transverse in and then lifting your buttocks. Your hands are holding ends of the scarf together on top of your belly. Rest your elbows on the floor. The exercise has three steps: (1) doing the pelvic tilt while in a supine position; (2) pulling the two halves of the recti together with the scarf; and (3) lifting your head as the transverse goes out your back to sixth floor. When you first start these exercises, it's good to have someone lift your head gently and check to be sure your transverse is going back, not forward. When you lift your head it's harder to hold that transverse muscle at fifth floor, and if it's going forward it is making your diastasis bigger. When lifting your head, bring your chin to your chest. Think that you're saying yes. Am I going to have an easy delivery? Think "yes" as you lift your head!

So let's start (see Figure 119):

1. Take a belly breath and bring your transverse to fifth floor, hold it there as you bring your pubic bone toward your navel in a pelvic tilt.

Figure 119 HEAD LIFTS:
Take a belly breath and bring the transverse to fifth floor. Hold it there as you bring your pubic bone toward your navel. Pull the ends of the sheet together. Bring your transverse out the back to sixth floor as you lift your head (chin to chest) and exhale, counting. Hold the transverse at fifth floor as you bring your pubic bone toward your navel.

Figure 120 WINDOW
STRETCH:
Sit down and cross one
leg over the other, rest-
ing one ankle on the
other knee. Hold the
transverse at fifth floor
as you lift the bottom
leg and put both hands
under that knee. Relax
the muscle and
breathe through the
stretch as you raise
your knee. Hold the
transverse at fifth floor
as you lower your foot
to the floor. Repeat
with the other leg.

2. Pull the ends of the sheet together.
3. Take that transverse out the back of your spine as you exhale and say "one." Close your eyes as you lift your head and touch your chin to your chest. Hold the transverse at fifth as you lower your head back to the floor.

Actually saying that number out loud will help you use your transverse muscle better. Also, if you're counting, you're exhaling, and if you're exhaling, you're breathing. Start with one set of 5 repetitions. Work up to 10, then 15, then 20, and finally 30. Do as many sets as you can. Your goal is three sets of 30 repetitions. (Remember to roll onto your side after each set, and while giving your abdominals a rest you can always get in some kegels.) I had a woman pregnant with twins who did three sets of 30 on the day she was supposed to deliver. She delivered two healthy 8-pound babies the next day and her abdominals got back in shape in almost no time.

Stretches

That's it! We're going to do a nice easy stretch now to cool down and ease those muscles that have been working hard.

Lie on your back and let's do the *window stretch* (see Figure 120). Cross your right leg over your left, resting your right ankle on your left knee. Hold that transverse in as you lift your left leg in the air. Now put both your hands under your left knee. Close your eyes and see that muscle you're stretching. See that muscle relax. You'll always relax a muscle before you stretch it.

Now breathe into the stretch. Expand the belly, take the transverse to your spine and hold it there as you bring your left knee toward your face and feel that muscle releasing and relaxing. Keep it there as you do one more stretch. Expand the belly, take the transverse to your spine and hold it there as you bring your left knee just a little closer to you and see that muscle releasing and relaxing. Now hold that transverse in as you put your foot on the floor. Now do the other leg.

Place both feet flat on the floor. Let's do an *inner thigh stretch* (see Figure 121). Hold that transverse in as you lift both knees toward your chest. Spread your knees and put your hands on your inner thighs. Now close your eyes and see those muscles relaxing. Always remember to relax the muscles before you stretch them. Now breathe through the stretch. Expand the belly, transverse to the spine, hold it there as you gently spread your thighs and see those muscles lengthening. Go nice and easy— don't overstretch these muscles. Now hold that transverse in as you bring your knees together, and hold your transverse at fifth floor as you put your feet on the floor.

Now, let's do a *back stretch* (see Figure 122). Bend your knees, keep your feet on the floor, and extend your arms. Your arms will never go above your shoulders. Now expand the belly, bring the transverse to fifth floor, and hold it there as you slowly roll your knees over to the left side. Make sure you keep your feet on the floor. Turn your head and look over your right shoulder. Now take two belly breaths. Expand the belly, exhale, and bring the belly to the spine. Once again. Expand the belly, exhale, and bring the belly to the spine. Hold that transverse at fifth floor and bring those knees back to the starting position. Now let's do the other

Figure 121 INNER THIGH STRETCH: Lie on your back and hold the transverse at fifth floor as you raise your knees. Spread your knees with your hands. Relax the muscles. Now breathe through the stretch as you press your legs open wider. Bring your knees together. Hold the transverse at fifth floor as you put your feet on the floor.

Figure 122 BACK STRETCH: Lie on your back with your bent knees together. Hold the transverse at fifth floor and keep your feet on the floor as you slowly roll your knees over to one side. Now turn your head and look over your other shoulder. Take a few belly breaths. Now hold transverse at fifth floor and return your knees to the starting position. Do the other side.

side. Expand the belly, transverse to fifth floor, hold it there as you slowly roll your knees to the right side. Make sure you keep your feet on the floor. Turn your head and look over your left shoulder. Now take two belly breaths. Expand the belly, exhale, and bring that transverse to the spine. Once again. Expand the belly, exhale, and bring the belly back to the spine. Now hold it there on the work of bringing the knees back to their starting position.

Roll over to your left side, and now just lie there for a moment. At this point I end the session by leading my client through a relaxation and birth visualization. (More about these relaxation techniques in the next chapter.) You might want to listen to some soothing music, take ten or fifteen minutes to relax, and focus on your pregnancy, birth, and baby. If you don't have time, then just congratulate yourself for working hard. Enjoy the feeling of your tired but strong muscles, the feeling of your powerful pregnant body that you're preparing for the marathon of labor.

Standing Warm-Up

arm stretches

upper back
stretches

lower back
stretches

side stretches

elbow rolls

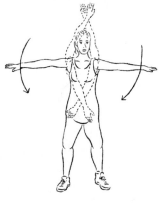

windmills

neck stretches

chin backs

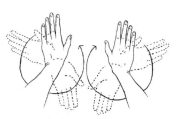

wrist circles

Standing Warm-Up

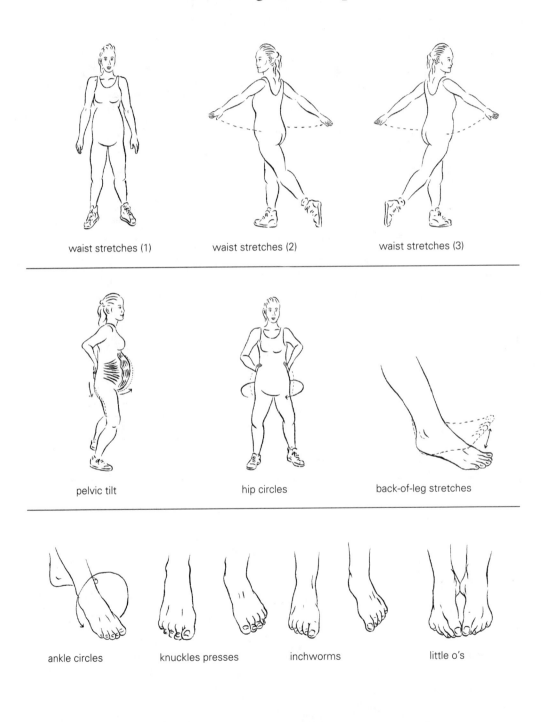

waist stretches (1)   waist stretches (2)   waist stretches (3)

pelvic tilt   hip circles   back-of-leg stretches

ankle circles   knuckles presses   inchworms   little o's

Hands and Knees

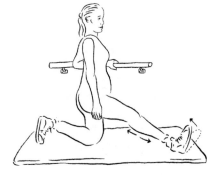

runner's stretch

back-of-leg stretches

pelvic tilt

side stretches

push-ups

elevators

supported squat

Seated Warm-Up

back-of-leg stretch (1)

back-of-leg stretch (2)

elevators (1)

elevators (2)

contracting

consider using a splint

Upper Body

upper body
stretches I (1)

upper body
stretches I (2)

upper body
stretches II

military
presses (1)

military
presses (2)

table tops (1)

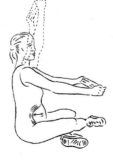

table tops (2)

forward pulls

ups and downs

Upper Body

overhead pulls (1)

overhead pulls (2)

lat pull-downs (1)

lat pull-downs (2)

rowing (1)

rowing (2)

Legs

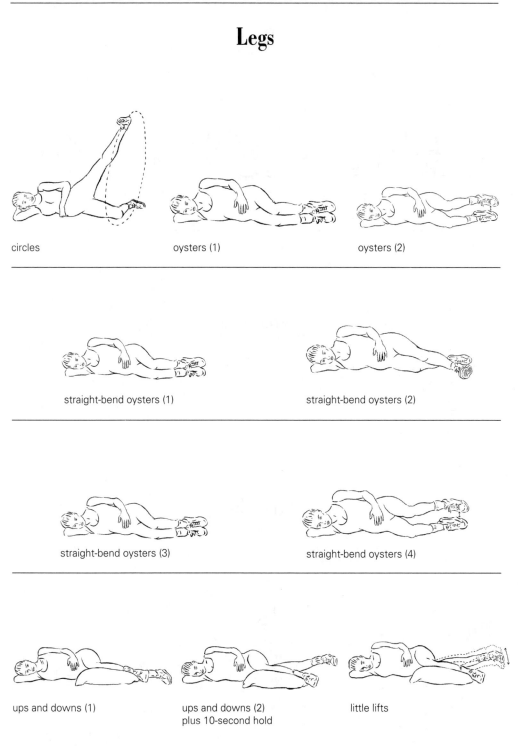

circles

oysters (1)

oysters (2)

straight-bend oysters (1)

straight-bend oysters (2)

straight-bend oysters (3)

straight-bend oysters (4)

ups and downs (1)

ups and downs (2)
plus 10-second hold

little lifts

Back

contracting   pelvic tilt (1)   pelvic tilt (2)

note: first work one
side of the LEGS, then
do BACK, then work
other side of LEGS,
then do head lift

pelvic tilt (3)   head lift

Stretches

window   inner thigh   back

CHAPTER 9

Relaxation and Visualization

When I finish a one-on-one workout with a client, I lead her through an exercise in mental relaxation and imaging. It's a way to help her feel soothed and calm and enjoy the feeling of resting the muscles that she's exercised. It's also a way to reinforce and practice that mind-body connection that I've been talking about throughout this book. This exercise includes a mental preview—a creative visualization—of the coming event, when she will be engaged in her marathon of labor, and how she will want to be working her mind and her body to deliver her baby into the world.

Harnessing mental powers to affect bodily responses is a well-established, medically sound technique. Simply relaxing and meditating—clearing the mind of jarring thoughts and the pressing concerns of daily life, and focusing on a soothing image or repeated phrase—can actually slow the heart rate and lower blood pressure.

Creative visualization, or mental imaging, takes the process a step further. In that same relaxed, calm state, picture yourself engaged in a future activity, imagine how it will feel and how you will be, and *see* yourself succeeding! Sports psychologists often make creative visualization part of an athlete's training. If you picture yourself executing the perfect golf drive, see your body move through each stage of the stroke from beginning to end, you will program your mind for success. This technique works!

Why not use creative visualization to rehearse for the greatest event you'll ever enter? You've been priming your muscles to get ready for birth, and you have "seen" those muscles getting stronger and more completely under your control. Now let's take some time to prepare your mind. In a sense, this is another flash-forward to the big day, but quite the opposite of the one we did in Chapter 4. This is you and your baby and nobody else. It's just the two of you—one of you giving birth, the other being born.

I've rarely known a pregnant woman who didn't experience some measure of trepidation about impending childbirth. This is normal and totally understandable. You're concerned about the pain, about whether the baby will be all right, about whether you will be all right. Creative visualization is a trial run that can help you relax, reduce your fears, and enjoy a welcoming, positive image of the birth experience.

Here is an abbreviated form of a favorite visualization I use with clients:

- Become aware of your breathing. Concentrate totally on the air coming in and going out of your body.
- Imagine that your breath contains a soft golden light, and admit that light into your womb to surround your baby.
- Imagine that golden light radiating out of your womb and filling your body. See the light moving down from your face through your jaws and your back and to your pelvis and down your legs, and see all those parts of your body feeling relaxed and free of all tension.
- Imagine that you can look into your womb and see your baby nestled there in perfect health and harmony. Tell yourself that you are giving your baby all he or she needs to be perfectly healthy and that your body has all it needs to labor and deliver your child into the world.
- Picture yourself now on a beautiful golden beach, and then see yourself floating on the water's surface, perfectly safe.
- See the waves surge higher and higher as you breathe more deeply and surrender to those waves. They are waves of energy and power. They circle your waist and tighten around your belly. The waves push your baby down and you welcome them.
- Imagine your cervix opening and feel your baby's head as it slides down and through.
- Imagine yourself after the waves have stopped. See yourself and your baby and your partner on the shore, warm and relaxed, filled with love, grateful to be together.
- Tell your baby how glad you are that he is here.

That's a summary of what we do. During this visualization I talk in a quiet and soothing voice as I lead my client through a much more elaborate, detailed description of the images above, with music. She pictures her body going through her baby's birth, her body doing what it is perfectly capable of doing and ready to do. The pregnant women I've worked with invariably *love* this part of the session, even the ones who start out being skeptical and wondering what on earth I'm talking about.

You can try relaxation and visual imaging at home by yourself. Remember, it's just as important to practice relaxation as it is to practice pushing, so that it will have become second nature to you when you get to labor. Here are some guidelines:

1. Begin your visualization by focusing on your breathing, which becomes deeper and slower.
2. Continue your visualization by directing your mind to the various parts of your body. See and feel them relax and become calm.
3. Include affirmations or positive suggestions throughout your visualizations. You might want to say to your baby in the womb, "I am taking good care of you and of myself. I am so happy that soon you'll be born." Or say to yourself, "My body is strong and my muscles are ready. I have love to give to my child, and my labor will be a labor of love."
4. Picture yourself going through the contractions of labor and acknowledge the tightness and pressure. See yourself perspiring, and see your baby moving down the birth canal. See your goal accomplished, and imagine yourself holding your baby in your arms.
5. Create your own visualization by using images that you find relaxing, comforting, and sustaining. In order for your visualization to be effective, the images should have meaning for you. Design a visualization that is filled with sensory details that feel positive and right to you, that lead you toward your goal.
6. Think of your goal—the safe, confident, joyous birth of your wonderful child—and picture yourself going through all the steps and accomplishing that goal.
7. You may want to use our "Coming Contractions" pain-management tape with our breathing and birthing visualizations (see Resources, at the back of this book), or another commercially prepared visualization tape. If you're into music, you may want to put together your own selections of favorite soothing tunes or sounds.

When you have created a visualization that suits you, talk it into your cassette recorder, perhaps with some soothing music in the background. And then try a little creative visualization when you've concluded your workout. Lower the lights and unplug the phone. No interruptions. Lie on your left side on the floor mat or on your bed, put one pillow under your head and one between your legs (to support the joints comfortably). Pop in your tape and let your mind travel to the grand day coming up, the day when all this fine work you've done for nine months will be so splendidly rewarded.

CHAPTER 10

Your Marathon of Labor

Here Comes Your Baby!

The big day has finally come. You are now in labor. You have trained your mind and your body during your pregnancy. You are strong, you feel empowered, and you are ready for your marathon of labor.

Labor, for all intents and purposes, occurs in two stages. You will deal with the pain in stage one as your cervix dilates, and you'll push your baby out with your abdominal muscles in stage two.

Relaxation, as we discussed in Chapter 9, is a key part of dealing with the pain of the first stage of labor. You've learned the skill of relaxation. You've been practicing throughout your pregnancy by listening to our "Coming Contractions" tape or to your own tape every day. Bring your tape with you to the hospital, along with a tape player. Don't forget to bring batteries; the hospital will not let you plug anything into the wall sockets! During the first stage of labor, play your tape, and your body will automatically relax.

During this first stage, the combination of gravity and the weight of the baby on your cervix will cause the cervix to open faster. Therefore, walking as much as possible in between contractions will help your labor progress. My clients have told me that pelvic tilts and belly dancing have felt good to them during this time. Many doctors are now using shorter-acting epidurals for those women who decide to have an epidural, and you will already have discussed with your obstetrician your preference for this kind of medication. If you do receive a short-acting epidural now to help you through stage one of labor, the medication should have worn off by the time you are ready to push, and you will be able to use your legs to squat or to get into another position where you need to use your legs.

For more suggestions on how to get through first-stage labor as comfortably and efficiently as possible, read Adrienne Lieberman's book *Easing Labor Pain* and Penny Simkin's *The Birth Partner.* I recommend these books to all my clients and to my trainers. (For more information, see the Resources section at the back of this book.)

You've now been told that you're 100 percent dilated and ready to deliver. You are now in stage two of labor. As we discussed earlier, the position you are in while pushing is just as important as your ability to push. Squatting is by far the best position, because your pelvis opens up 27 percent more than if you were flat on your back, and your uterus is in a gravity-friendly position. It's easier to push with your abdominals when you're sitting up than it is when you're lying on your back. If your hospital or birthing center will accommodate a squatting delivery, you are in an ideal situation to sail through stage two labor. You've practiced your supported squat for five minutes every day during your pregnancy, so you're ready to use this position to get that baby out as fast as possible! You've strengthened your abdominals, your knees, and your pelvic floor muscles, and you've stretched your pelvic floor muscles and your lower back. You can squat in any of several ways; hold on to a squatting bar; sit on a squatting stool (see the Resources section); have your partner and a nurse support you under your arms in this position; or hold on to the foot of the hospital bed.

Other acceptable positions for pushing are (1) on your hands and knees, where you can do your pelvic tilts to help your lower back; and (2) lying on your side. As you know, lying on your back with your legs pulled back is *not* a good position, because your pelvis does not open up and your uterus is not in a gravity-assisted position. Also, it's harder to push with your abdominals when you're lying on your back, as you discovered when doing your head lifts in Chapter 8. The supine position is also very hard on your pelvic floor muscles; it puts too much pressure on your venae cavae. If you *do* end up on your back, however, the abdominal exercises you've been doing throughout your pregnancy will definitely be helpful. Many of my clients have delivered in this position and had success pushing with their strengthened abdominals.

So you're in position now and you're ready to push. You've practiced this pushing technique every morning while having a bowel movement, and of course you've been strengthening your upper and lower body by doing the Maternal Fitness routine. The transverse exercises have become second nature to you, and your abdominal muscles are strong. You have also explained this technique to your partners, and they are prepared to support your breathing and pushing in case you are told to hold your breath. So you close your eyes and think of that image of pushing, like squeezing on a tube of toothpaste—transverse pressing back against the uterus while your strengthened pelvic floor muscles are open and relaxed. You have learned during your exercising to isolate and separate those two muscles so that when the abdominals are tight and pushing, the pelvic floor muscles are open and relaxed.

As you feel a contraction begin, take a belly breath and expand your belly. Now bring that transverse to the spine and then out the back as you vocalize (count, moan, swear, sing opera). Feel that pelvic floor opening like a flower. Remember—no breath holding! Always exhale, pushing with your strengthened abdominal muscles.

Here are some comments from women—including an obstetrician—who found that their Maternal Fitness workouts empowered them for the marathon of labor:

Ellie McGrath, marathon runner and new mom: "During my pregnancy I worked on preparing the muscles that would be most important during the actual childbirth. I worked with Maternal Fitness on the transverse abdominal muscles and practiced breathing properly. When I did go into labor, the work paid off. At just over an hour, my doctor assumed that I must be too tired to continue doing three sets of ten pushes at a time. When she asked if I wanted to go down to two sets, I told her that I'd prefer to move up to four. The baby was born soon after. My doctor was impressed with how strong I was. I think the Maternal Fitness program is an excellent combination of exercise, education, and relaxation. Taking part in the program was one of the best decisions I made. I attribute my good recovery from childbirth to the fact that I maintained optimal fitness during my pregnancy."

Dr. Ellen Manos, obstetrician: "Maternal Fitness has a great method of communicating information to their clients so that the women they train feel in control of their bodies, both during and after pregnancy. The program has helped to make a difficult and often frightening experience not only manageable but enjoyable. I can say this with absolute assurance, since I was one of their clients. The coaching in abdominal wall strengthening and control played a large role in my wonderful delivery of Zoe Eleni on April 7, 1993."

Stephanie Young, health and fitness editor of *Glamour* magazine: "As a journalist, I interviewed Julie Tupler about her Maternal Fitness program and featured her information on pushing on the Health and Pregnancy page of *Glamour* magazine. The Maternal Fitness program made a big difference in my pregnancy and birthing experience [when I was] a mother-to-be for the second time. I felt great—very strong and energetic—throughout my pregnancy and into my delivery. No backaches as in my first pregnancy. My obstetrician, labor nurse, and a medical student who observed my birth were very impressed with my labor and delivery. As the medical student remarked, "I've never seen a more controlled labor." And it's true. Maternal Fitness had prepared me both physically and psychologically for labor."

I hope you will stick with the Maternal Fitness workouts throughout your pregnancy. And remember that once your baby has arrived, all the good workouts you've been giving your body will continue to pay off! The benefits you derive from strong, flexible muscles and proper breathing won't disappear once you've become a mother.

You'll have an easier, faster post-birth recovery if you start doing your transverse and kegel exercises again right after your baby is born. You'll be able to carry your baby comfortably, because the exercises you've been doing over the past months have strengthened and toned the muscles that you need to do all that satisfying but *tiring* work! Some of my clients begin doing the exercises about one week after they deliver, focusing on kegels and transverse contracting. You can do these while you're sitting down and feeding the baby. Wait until you feel ready to go, and then work back up to your pre-delivery workout schedule. You'll get there faster than you think if you did the program regularly.

In fact, keep up your Maternal Fitness exercise routine, and it will help you all through your marathon of parenthood!

CHAPTER 11

More Fitness Factors

All You Really Need to Know About Eating Right During Pregnancy

You know that while you're pregnant you're eating for two. You know that what you feed yourself you're also feeding your baby. Now I want us to get a little more specific about this business of food and nourishment, and how what you eat and drink affects what's going on inside your pregnant body.

If you've stayed with me this far, you're already an expert on your muscles. Now you'll get to know some organs and body tissues that are of major significance in the physiology of pregnancy. Caring for them through proper nutrition is as big a part of maternal fitness as is working your muscles and developing strength from the center for your marathon of labor. It's time now for another brief anatomy course.

Anatomy 201

Once the sperm and the egg get together, your body sets in motion a masterfully designed mechanism geared toward producing a baby. You've grown a new organ that will do in utero what you'll be doing on the outside after your baby is born—in effect, feeding, nurturing, and changing diapers! And some other organs and systems that are already in place will start working hard to get your body utilizing the good stuff, getting rid of the bad stuff, and accommodating the needs of that new life.

Here are some of the developments that are going on:

You grow a placenta. The placenta is a spongy organ that begins to form inside the uterus in the first weeks of pregnancy and that, toward the end, weighs about 1½ pounds and looks rather like raw liver. It exists for the sole purposes of getting nutrients and oxygen from your body into your baby's body and getting wastes from your baby into your circulatory system so they can be eliminated. After your baby is born, the placenta's usefulness is over, and in a vaginal birth it is discharged through the vagina. This is called the third stage of labor, and I'm glad the placenta has a stage all its own, because it deserves one.

I love the placenta almost as much as I love the transverse muscle! I admire its short, focused, hardworking life! Here's how this hardy little organ works: The placenta grows from nutrients it gets from your bloodstream through the uterine lining. One of its surfaces affixes itself to the uterine lining. Another surface is connected to your baby through the umbilical cord. Capillaries, those tiniest of blood vessels, make possible the nutrient-waste exchange. I picture this marvelous circulatory mechanism as little arms reaching from mother to baby and from baby to mother—giving life, growing life.

The walls of your uterus get thick. For years your uterus has been sitting there waiting to go into action. Now that you're pregnant, it's ready to go. If you've been generally taking good care of yourself and you are in good health, the lining of your uterus (the endometrium) is primed to let the placenta dig in and make a firm implantation.

Before you had a baby growing in there, your uterus was a slight little thing weighing a scant few ounces. Over the course of your pregnancy it gets big and tough and eventually weighs about two pounds. It needs to grow in order to help the placenta do its job and to cushion your baby safely. How well it develops during these nine months has to do with how well—that is, how nutritiously—you're feeding yourself.

You make more blood. A lot more. If you're an average-sized woman—before pregnancy normally weighing around 130 pounds—you have about 3½ quarts of blood. By your twenty-eighth to thirtieth week of pregnancy you will have added over 2 quarts to that! Most of this added volume is in the form of plasma, the fluid part of the blood. You're making more red cells, too, but not as many, so they become diluted. That, as you may already know, is called physiologic anemia of pregnancy, and it's one of the reasons you may feel tired.

What's the reason for having all this extra blood? Again, your body is doing what it knows it should do to keep the pregnancy mechanism running like clockwork. More blood in your system encourages the placenta to grow and facilitates that amazing, life-producing transfer of nutrients and oxygen and waste products between mother and baby. You'll have the greatest amount of blood during the last trimester, just when your baby needs to put on weight and store nutrients so as to thrive after birth. Having a greater volume of blood also helps protect the pregnant woman from difficulties if she should bleed a lot during birth.

Your body has figured out some ingenious ways to keep producing and maintaining 50 to 60 percent more blood than you need. For one thing, your heart rate increases to keep all that blood in circulation. For another, you may start craving salty food. Your body wants you to take in a good supply of dietary salt because salt helps pull water out of the tissues and retain it in the bloodstream, and that's what increases the amount of plasma. For another, your renal tract will dilate so that it can hold more urine, making you urinate more frequently and thus get thirstier and drink more than usual—and thus get extra fluid into your system.

Your liver goes into overtime. Your liver *really* gets down to work now. That wonderful organ is functioning in several important ways to ensure a healthy pregnancy. Recognizing the need for more blood, your liver produces protein molecules, primarily albumin, that pull fluid out to the tissues and into the bloodstream. And remember this: your liver can make albumin only from the protein you eat, so you'll need to eat the right amount of protein-rich foods.

But that's not all the liver does. You know that your hormones are running riot, which is part of what's causing the queasiness, the constipation, the tiredness, and some of those other nasty symptoms. But do you know just how much of these hormones your pregnant body is producing? Your hormone levels can rise to the equivalent of taking one hundred birth controls pills a day! Your body doesn't want or need all those hormones, however, and that's where the liver comes in. It clears out hormones by converting them into products that your kidneys can get rid of.

Here's something else your liver is working at. Your body always has some toxins inside it. They may have entered from the environment or been produced naturally by the lower bowel as waste products. During pregnancy your digestion slows down. This is good because it helps nutrients be fully absorbed, but slower digestion also means that toxic by-products have a more favorable environment in which to develop. That means your liver has to work harder to metabolize those toxins and get rid of them.

Your Diet

So what does all this have to do with what you're going to eat for breakfast this morning or for dinner tonight? Everything! How and what you eat determines how successfully this wonderfully intricate and powerful pregnancy machinery works. I want you to think about feeding your uterus, feeding your blood, feeding your placenta, and feeding your liver. You can enable them to do their work by giving them the raw materials they need.

What will your doctor tell you about food? Not much. I ask my clients what they've learned from their doctors about nutrition and pregnancy. The great majority tell me either that their doctors haven't talked about this subject at all or that they were handed a pamphlet about eating for two and were given the name of a multivitamin supplement.

The assumption on the part of these medical professionals, I guess, is that if your vitals—that is, your blood pressure and urine and so on—are okay and you're gaining weight, you must be eating adequately. Or maybe doctors assume that we've all heard so much about the importance of getting a balanced diet that no more need be said. Or perhaps they believe that their job is to be on call for the big day or if anything goes wrong beforehand, and you and your body will just naturally see to all the rest.

In the matter of nutrition, then, *you* have to get yourself informed and take charge of what you need to do for yourself and your baby during these nine months. And then, as an informed consumer, you should go to your doctor, talk over your eating plans with him or her, and together work out any adjustments that might be needed based on your medical history, your pre-pregnancy weight-to-height ratio, and the results of your monthly checkups. You may also want to ask to be referred to a nutritionist.

A word about those multivitamin and mineral supplements: I'm not a big fan of popping pills if you can get what your body needs through a nutritious diet. During pregnancy you do require more than normal amounts of certain nutrients—iron, folic acid, and calcium, for example—and taking supplements is one way of ensuring an adequate intake. But thinking that swallowing a little tablet each day is all you have to do to make up for whatever's missing in your diet is the wrong way to go. Those supplements can't give you extra protein or calories, something you need during pregnancy. And too many vitamins or the wrong combinations can even be harmful—for example, too much vitamin A can be toxic.

Besides, good food will do wonders for you! Study the next few pages, analyze your diet in the ways I'll show you, and make any necessary adjustments.

Eleven Things You Need to Know About Eating During Pregnancy

Here are some general guidelines and words of wisdom to keep in mind as you figure out what, when, and how to eat during these nine months:

1. Figure on gaining weight. We've come a long way in recent decades in reversing old notions of what was "good" or "healthy" weight gain in a pregnant woman. Years ago doctors chastised a woman who put on more than 15 or so pounds. Part of this notion dated back to a time when many women died in childbirth, when cesareans were rare, and when it was believed that if the mother ate less during her pregnancy she would produce a smaller—and thus more easily deliverable—baby. It was also mistakenly thought that limited weight gain would help prevent toxemia, a potentially deadly disease that occurs when liver metabolism breaks down.

Doctors know better now, and so do we women. For one thing, it's a documented fact that smaller babies have more difficulties after birth. And the added pounds we put on during pregnancy mean stored-up calories, a protection the body can call on if a woman gets sick or nauseated or temporarily reduces her food intake for some other reason.

Most obstetricians now will encourage a weight gain of 25 to 35 pounds, and an even greater gain can be perfectly normal and appropriate for certain women. You are unique. Your body is unique. And as long as you are putting on the pounds from eating wholesome, nutritious foods and not from junk foods, your body will gain what it needs to support your pregnancy.

2. Never diet. *Do* figure out a healthy eating pattern. *Do not* attempt to lose weight during these months. That's important. I've worked with clients who have started their pregnancies as large, overweight women, and I've seen how alarmed they can get about the prospect of packing on even more pounds.

This is not the time to distract yourself with worries about being fat. (And if you're a fitness fanatic, don't think of exercising during pregnancy as a means of weight control.) What may happen, though, as you change your eating habits to eliminate the junk and incorporate the healthy foods is that you may find yourself spontaneously reducing. That's just fine for you and your baby.

3. Take in more calories. You need calories to give you the energy your body needs to make your baby. In fact, your body will need about 55,000 extra calories to bring your child through the nine months of growing inside you and moving healthily out into the world.

Doctors and pregnancy nutritionists recommend that this extra calorie intake be concentrated in the last two-thirds of your pregnancy, which means that you should be taking in 300 added calories a day during your second and third trimesters. If you're an average-sized woman, that means you'll need to consume 2,400 to 2,600 total calories daily. If you don't get enough calories, your body will burn up protein instead, and that means less protein is available to stoke the pregnancy machinery.

Perhaps you think it'll be easy to scarf down an extra 300 calories a day. A couple of chocolate chip cookies? A wedge of cheesecake with cherry topping? Well, that's not the best way to go. Calories from those sources are running on empty, and during pregnancy it's especially important not to be overcaloried and undernourished. Choose nutrient-dense foods—foods that offer high-quality nutrient value per calorie (more later about what those good foods are).

4. Eat often and regularly. I've frequently had clients tell me they're just not very hungry a lot of the time or are bothered by queasiness and nausea. But it's critical to keep eating regularly and well, and in fact, taking in more food can help dispel the nausea. But it's critical to keep eating regularly and well, and in fact, taking in more food can help dispel the nausea by keeping your blood sugar stable. Usually your appetite will improve after the first trimester.

If you're turned off by a full dinner plate, eat small, frequent meals throughout the day. Try to eat three regular meals and two or three snacks. You can eat before going to bed or when you wake up in the middle of the night, if that feels comfortable to you.

5. Drink more fluids than you normally do. Remember that blood volume that needs to get pumped up. Your body has set things up so that you're probably urinating more and drinking more anyway, but keep in mind that you need to drink at least sixty-four ounces of fluid a day. If you're very active or a regular exerciser—and especially if it's summertime or if you live in a hot and humid climate—increase your intake even more.

Drinking juice and milk is a good way to get fluid. Fruit juices and milk, however, have many more calories than water. Water of course, is always terrific and calorie free. And if you haven't already done so, I recommend that after your first trimester you sample the pleasures and benefits of red raspberry leaf tea, which is available at most health food stores. It's safe, it's soothing, it contains a rich concentration of good vitamins and easily assimilated calcium and iron, and it gives tone to the muscles of the uterus.

6. If you want salt, have salt. We all tend to think that salt is a big no-no, and many doctors still advise their pregnant patients to cut back on it. If you are being monitored by your doctor for high blood pressure or kidney problems, you should talk to him or her about your salt intake. But if you have no such special considerations, this substance is vital to the pregnancy machinery that's working at getting fluid out of the body's tissues and into the bloodstream.

Listen to your body and eat accordingly. If you are following a healthy diet, it is difficult to take in too much salt, because what isn't needed will be excreted by your

---

Water, Water, Water

Water really is the best thing you can drink at any time, but especially when you're pregnant. Here's what drinking water does for you:

- It cools you down. Your core body temperature is higher than normal during these nine months, and it's especially important to avoid getting overheated. So cooling down by drinking lots of water should be part of your daily routine.
- Water helps maintain your body's fluids. Whenever you sweat, you lose water, and water helps keep all your organs functioning properly. Most important during these months, drinking water helps keep amniotic fluid levels up.
- It also helps the placenta to grow, and a healthy, well-nourished placenta gets nutrients to your baby and helps prevent toxemia.
- Water has zero calories. Pregnancy is not a time to count calories or fret about weight gain, but you do want to avoid the empty calories that come with sodas and other soft drinks.

kidneys. You can get too *little* salt, however, if you intentionally restrict your intake, and that can lead to disrupted liver function, elevated blood pressure, and edema, or accumulation of fluid in cells and tissues.

7. Think protein, calcium, iron, vitamin C, and folic acid. These are the essential building blocks for the new life you're growing, and during these nine months you will want to make sure that the food you eat is supplying your body with adequate amounts of them.

Even if you've always been a pretty decent eater who tried to maintain a balanced diet, you will still need to increase your intake of dietary protein, calcium, and iron. Your growing baby is sucking up protein and calcium to produce the billions of cells needed for organs and bones and a heart and a brain and all the rest of the baby's healthy new body.

In addition to protein and calcium, you need iron to keep all that extra blood functioning right and to supply your baby's needs. If you don't get enough iron through your diet, your baby will draw iron from *your* body stores and set you up as a potential candidate for anemia.

We all think of vitamin C when we have a cold, but it also acts as a cementing agent that holds new cells together. Plus, it helps your body absorb calcium and iron more efficiently, so it's good to eat and combine foods that are high in vitamin C and iron.

Folic acid is one of the B vitamins, and pregnant women who get enough of it through their food decrease their babies' chances of developing certain birth defects. You'll see later on which foods are especially good sources of protein, calcium, iron, vitamin C, and folic acid, but for now just remember that you need more than the usual amount of this good stuff.

8. When you crave something sweet—and you will—go for protein instead of sugar. As you know, you need a good supply of protein coming in. Besides, when your body is signaling through a craving for sweets that your glucose, or blood sugar, levels need to be raised, protein-rich foods—cheese and crackers, for example—will do the job more steadily and nutritiously than sugary foods, though perhaps not as quickly. Choose the protein, and then if you still want something sweet, eat an apple, a peach, or a bowl of strawberries. (Fresh fruits help ward off constipation, too.)

9. Go natural. Eat whole grain breads, fresh fruits and vegetables, and lean meats, cooked and prepared simply. Choose good, nutrient-rich ingredients that are not processed, that are not canned (except fish), and that have few additives.

10. Enjoy a wide variety of foods. Maybe you've never tried kale (a good source of folic acid) or sardines (a great source of calcium). Maybe now's the time. You need many different foods during these nine months, as you look over the food lists later, see how you might incorporate a variety of high-quality items into your menu.

Pregnancy *isn't* a good time, however, to pull a major switcheroo in your eating habits—no time to go macrobiotic, for example, or start adding chicken or meat if you've been vegetarian for some time, or to drink milk if you know that dairy foods are a problem for you. Your body may have difficulty tolerating unaccustomed foods, and you can find substitutes that will supply the nutrients you need.

11. Watch what you drink. I strongly advise you to drink *no alcohol at all* during the first trimester, and limited alcohol, if any, after that.

Eliminate your consumption of caffeine (found in caffeinated coffee, tea, and colas) during the first trimester, and reduce it after that. Caffeine crosses the placenta and gets to your baby (it also enters breast milk), and that's not great. There are also indications that pregnant women who drink more than one or two cups of coffee a day have a slightly higher risk of miscarriage. Coffee may pose a special problem not only because of the caffeine but also because of chemicals released during the roasting process. Be on the safe side while you're pregnant.

Where Do You Stand?

You may be eating well right now. Or you may be taking in more junky stuff or just-not-great stuff than you realize. Or you may have an all-purpose, nicely balanced diet that's still coming up a little short on some of those extras you need during pregnancy.

It's helpful to get your eating habits down in black and white, so you can see exactly what you really are consuming and then consider what changes might be in order. Keep a food diary for three nonconsecutive days, a little chart on which you write down everything you eat. That includes the bag of chips at your desk and the spoonfuls of ice cream out of the container while you're standing at the refrigerator in the middle of the night. Write down all of the following:

- What foods you eat.
- How much of it you eat. Some things are easy, like one slice of bread or one slice of pizza. But you'll also get good at estimating amounts: a half cup of pasta, three-quarters of a cup of cereal, four ounces of chicken, or a half cup (eight spoonfuls)

of ice cream. For a day or two, measure out portions and then you'll know by sight how much is how much. Here's a simple way to recognize a four-ounce portion of meat, chicken, or fish: it's about as big around as your palm and as thick as the point where your pinky is attached to your hand.

- Whether a particular food is fresh, frozen, or canned. Choose fresh foods whenever possible. Frozen foods are okay, but canned products, for the most part, should be out.
- What and how much liquid you drink.

Look over your three days' worth of eating and, based on our eleven guidelines and on the lists of foods and recommended daily menus below, make the adjustments that will provide the best fuel for that baby-making machinery.

A Pregnancy Diet: What You Should Eat Each Day

Here are the five food categories and roughly how much you need each day from each category. The portions given with each food equal one serving. Choose whole grains over refined grains—for example, brown rice and bread over white rice and bread.

- **Grains (6 to 11 servings)**
  1 slice enriched or whole grain bread
  ½ bagel
  ½ English muffin
  ½ hamburger bun
  2 puffed rice cakes
  6 soda crackers
  1 graham cracker (all four quarters)
  ½ matzo (a 2-by-3-inch portion)
  5 buttery snack-type crackers
  ¾ cup dry cereal
  ½ cup cooked cereal
  ½ cup cooked rice, bulgur, couscous
  ½ cup cooked pasta

- **Fruits (at least 2 servings)**

  1 cup fresh mixed fruits

  1 medium-sized serving fresh fruit (1 apple, 1 banana, 1 orange, etc.; or ¼ cantaloupe; ¼ avocado)

  ¾ cup fruit juice

- **Vegetables (at least 3 servings)**

  ½ cup cooked (preferably steamed) vegetables (including a yellow or orange vegetable 5 times a week)

  1 cup raw leafy green or yellow vegetables

  ¾ cup vegetable juice

- **Protein (at least 6–8 ounces)**

  1 egg = 1 ounce of protein

  boneless meat, fish, or skinless poultry; a piece about the size of your palm and as thick as the point where your pinky is attached to your hand = 4 ounces of protein

  ½ cup fish (including canned tuna, salmon, and sardines) = 3–4 ounces of protein

  1 cup cooked dried beans of any variety = 2 ounces of protein

  2 tablespoons peanut butter = 1 ounce of protein

  6 ounces of tofu = 2 ounces of protein

- **Calcium-rich foods (at least 4 servings)**

  1½ ounces hard cheese

  1 cup milk (skim, 1%, or 2%)

  1 cup yogurt

  ¼ cup cottage cheese

  1½ cups soy milk

  4 ounces tofu

You need a *little* fat and oil, too. Remember, you get these in many foods, especially peanut butter, nuts, butter, salad dressings, some sauces, and foods that are cooked in or with oil. Use olive or canola oil whenever possible.

The Good Food List

Here are some foods that are especially rich in those nutrients that the pregnant body especially needs:

Protein	Calcium	Iron	Vitamin C	Folic Acid
eggs	cheese	eggs	broccoli	asparagus
cheese (high	milk	fish	cantaloupe	broccoli
in fat)	custard	beef	cauliflower	cashew nuts
fish	yogurt	liver	grapefruit	collard greens
lean meat	dark green leafy	poultry	oranges	lentils
poultry	vegetables	baked beans	orange juice	lima beans
dried beans	canned salmon or	blueberries	papaya	orange juice
and peas	sardines, with	prunes	peppers	peanuts
lentils	bones	raisins	baked potatoes	romaine lettuce
nuts	shrimp	spinach	strawberries	spinach
peanut butter	sesame seeds	sardines	tomatoes	wheat germ
(high in fat)	tofu	broccoli	watermelon	liver
tofu			kiwi	

That's it. All you really need to know about pregnancy and nutrition. As we mentioned, you'll quickly learn how to estimate the amount in a portion—how much broccoli is half a cupful or how big a piece of chicken breast is four ounces. But don't worry excessively about measuring or about what constitutes a serving or about figuring out calories. Pick good foods, eliminate junk foods, take in enough food at each meal to feel comfortable—neither hungry nor stuffed—eat healthy snacks, and you'll do just fine.

Resources

- Maternal Fitness Referral Service (for information on a program in your area or for Registered Nurses or Physical Therapists interested in franchising a program in your area): 212-353-1947 or visit our web site at www.maternalfitness.com or e-mail at jtupler@maternalfitness.com.

- Maternal Fitness Products: Send a check or money order made out to Maternal Fitness to 108 E. 16th Street, 4th Floor, New York, NY 10003 or order by phone or e-mail with a credit card for the products listed. Please add 8.25% sales tax if you live in New York. You may also order products directly from the manufacturers.
- *Coming Contractions* pain management tape for labor: $15.00 plus $2.00 shipping and handling.
- Dyna-Bands and light weights can be ordered through Fitness Wholesale: 800-532-5512. Light weights can also be found at most sporting goods stores.
- The Pregnancy Survival Kit by Belly Basics (a comfortable and fashionable four-piece wardrobe in a box): 800-4–9 Months or 800-496-6684.
- Squatting chair for use during labor by deBy Birth Supports: 603-332-7766, or The Family Life Center: 518-465-0241.
- Raspberry leaf tea is available at health food stores.
- Splint: $20 plus $5.00 for shipping and handling (to be used while exercising during pregnancy and worn immediately after birth).
- *Mom and Baby Progression Guide* and *Nutrition At-a-Glance:* Contact Momease at 877-666-3273.

Recommended Books

- Penny Simkin, P.T. *The Birth Partner.* Boston: Harvard Common Press, 1989.
- Sheila Kitzinger. *The Complete Book of Pregnancy.* New York: Knopf, 1989.
- Adrienne Lieberman. *Easing Labor Pain.* Boston: Harvard Common Press, 1992.
- Elizabeth Noble, P.T. *Essential Exercises for the Childbearing Year.* Boston: Houghton Mifflin, 1988.
- Elaine Stillerman. *Mother Massage.* New York: Bantam Doubleday Dell, 1992.
- Raul Artal. *Pregnancy and Exercise.* New York: Bantam Doubleday Dell, 1992.
- Mike Samuels and Nancy Samuels. *The New Well Pregnancy Book.* New York: Simon & Schuster, 1996.
- Connie Marshall, R.N.M.S.N., *From Here to Maternity.* Marshall Educational Solutions Inc., 1-800-428-8321, 1994.

INDEX

(Page numbers in *italic* refer to captions and illustrations.)

155